Berlitz®

rn
an

Barbados • St Lucia
St Vincent and the Grenadines
Grenada • Trinidad and Tobago

Berlitz

Southern Caribbean

Text by Suzanne Patterson
Editor: Earleen Brunner
Photography: Jürg Donatsch
Additional photography: Junia Browne (p8);
Bob Krist (p31); David Weintraub (p64)
Layout: Media Content Marketing, Inc.
Cartography by Apa Publications
Managing Editor: Tony Halliday

Fourth Edition 2002

CONTACTING THE EDITORS

Every effort has been made to provide accurate information in this publication, but changes are inevitable. The publisher cannot be responsible for any resulting loss, inconvenience or injury. We would appreciate it if readers would call our attention to any errors or outdated information by contacting Berlitz Publishing, PO Box 7910, London SE1 1WE, England. Fax: (44) 20 7403 0290;
e-mail: berlitz@apaguide.demon.co.uk

Printed in Singapore by Insight Print Services (Pte) Ltd, 38 Joo Koon Road, Singapore 628990. Tel: (65) 6865-1600. Fax: (65) 6861-6438

060/204 RP

CONTENTS

- A ☛ in the text denotes a highly recommended sight
- A complete A–Z of practical information starts on p.105
- Extensive mapping on cover flaps

SOUTHERN CARIBBEAN

THE ISLANDS AND THE PEOPLE

The Southern Caribbean islands are for escapists — who don't want to escape too far. They're not untouched Shangri-La waiting for a discoverer, but they have all the attributes. Lush tropical plants and flowers bloom year-round. Silvery, golden-white, or volcanic black sand beaches fringe the gentle Caribbean and wind-lashed Atlantic.

Glorious sunshine and sunsets washed in every color of a painter's palette add to the allure of the Southern Caribbean. The temperature seldom strays from the balmy range of 21° to 32°C (70° to 90°F). The rainy season officially extends from May to November, but showers rarely last very long. Hurricanes and other fierce tropical storms that can sweep devastatingly through the Caribbean in August and September pose the only real weather problem. Getting away from it all is not difficult on these small islands. They are strung out in an arc between the French West Indies and the Venezuelan coast, roughly 4,000 km (2,500 miles) south of New York. Even Trinidad, the largest of them, with more than 4,662 sqare km (1,800 square miles) is a mite compared with Jamaica or Cuba to the north.

Barbados, St. Lucia, St. Vincent, the Grenadines, Grenada, and Tobago and Trinidad are referred to here as the Southern Caribbean islands for the sake of convenience. They share the same geographical situation within the West Indies, and none of them are more than 100 miles apart.

Trinidad bears a geological similarity to Venezuela, from which it broke away in the distant past. Tobago rose from the sea in volcanic eruptions, as did St. Lucia, St. Vincent, and Grenada. Today, the volcanoes are mainly quiet tourist attractions, except for St. Vincent's, which erupted dramatically in

1979. Barbados, the easternmost of the Southern Caribbean group, was formed from deposits of coral and limestone, and this green and fertile isle always furnishes pure spring water.

Each island has its own distinctive history. Most of them were sighted by Christopher Columbus during his third voyage in 1498, but only Trinidad was claimed for Spain. It was the French and English who fought over and colonized the others, ousting the local Carib Indians in the process. This tribe waged a fierce battle for the area that now bears its name.

While pirates and buccaneers were creating havoc all over the Caribbean in the 18th century, sugar and slavery made rich planters of the adventurers who settled the islands. England gained the upper hand in the Southern Caribbean and eventually took all the islands for the crown.

Former slaves celebrate their freedom

Slavery was abolished in the 19th century. Small landholdings were worked by former slaves, and the thirst for independence grew. The islands became British Associated States, but all of them have now chosen total independence and self-government. Except for Grenada, the governments have been stable and democratically elected since independence.

About 90 per cent of the people who inhabit the Southern Caribbean islands are the black or mulatto descendants of African slaves.

Two young ladies of Trinidad beam a pleasant, understated welcome to visitors

However, Trinidad's polyglot population includes East Indians and Chinese. French patois is heard with English in St. Lucia.

Carnival costumes, an exuberant style of painting and dancing, and music, its sinuous rhythm inherited from Africa and influenced by Spain, are among the attractions of the islands. Some islands boast excellent composers, songwriters, poets, and playwrights. Trinidad-born V. S. Naipul has won international acclaim for his stories, essays, and novels, as has the St Lucian Derek Walcott for his poems and plays.

There are few high-rise developments in the Southern Caribbean, even on heavily populated Barbados. Brightly painted wooden houses with gingerbread ornament can be seen among new cement homes. Cars share road space with farm boys leading goats or carrying wicked-looking machetes for cutting sugar cane or chopping wood.

An English-style school system is only one of the legacies left to the islands by Great Britain. Driving is on the left; everybody speaks English, and government and administration follow the British pattern. Cricket and a general love of sport persist.

Whether you holiday at one of the sophisticated resorts on Barbados, or claim a beach for your own on Tobago, you'll enjoy the pleasures of sun and sea. Cruise in your own tiny sailboat, climb to the peak of a volcanic mountain, or paddle the shallows in search of colourful fish. Visit the Great House of an old plantation, or a botanic garden.

Barbados has a large, modern airport, and the island is fully geared to tourism. Others are moving at a somewhat slower pace. There are daily flights to the major tourist centres, with resort hotels of world class on most islands. Though few of the islands have escaped the tourist boom (mainly Dominica and St. Vincent), most are still relatively unspoilt. So relax and enjoy the sedate pace of life in the tropics.

St. Lucia's Castries Market does a brisk daily business.

A BRIEF HISTORY

Long before Columbus set out on his voyages of discovery, groups of Amerindians made their way from South America to the Southern Caribbean area. By A.D. 300 tribes of Arawaks, peaceful farmers and fishermen, were in residence on many islands.

Then, a hundred years or so before the first Spanish adventurers arrived, a warlike tribe swept up from South America, killing off the Arawaks and probably eating their flesh for ritualistic purposes, if not for food.

They called themselves Caribs (rendered in Spanish as *canibales*—"cannibals"), but the savage name later came to be given to the gentlest of turquoise seas and lushest of islands. The Caribs founded settlements on most of the Southern Caribbean islands.

Exploration and Colonization

Columbus sighted most of the Southern Caribbean islands on his third voyage in 1498, remarking on their beauty and then sailing on. Soon other Spaniards were in pursuit of treasure. They concentrated on Cuba, Mexico, and the South American mainland, using the Southern Caribbean islands principally as bases from which to search for the gold of El Dorado.

Only Trinidad was colonized by Spain, and the exploitation of the smaller islands was left to the English and French. By the early 16th century, the French, English, and Dutch had staked claims in the Southern Caribbean, bringing Spanish dominance of the area to an end. In the 1510s sugarcane was introduced into most of the islands, as well as a small trade in slaves, which was soon cornered by the Portuguese.

The French and English also indulged in smuggling and privateering—the appropriation of goods from ships of rival countries with the blessing of the home government. Throughout the 16th and 17th centuries, buccaneers from France and England plundered the region.

In 1562, an English privateer called John Hawkins broke the Portuguese monopoly on slave-trading by bringing slaves from the West African coast and selling them in the Caribbean. Shortly after that, in 1586, Sir Francis Drake sacked the town of Cartagena in Colombia in the name of the English Crown. Two years later, he and John Hawkins led forces to defeat the Spanish Armada—an event that marked Spain's gradual decline as a strong influence in the New World.

On the islands, the 17th century saw a boom in the production of sugarcane and the manufacture of rum. As refining mills

A dignified Columbus solemnly presides over Port-of-Spain in Trinidad.

were built, more and more slaves were imported from Africa—as many as 75,000 a year by the end of the 17th century. Their descendants would later rule most of the Caribbean.

Britain versus France

Except for Barbados, which never strayed from the British fold, the Southern Caribbean islands changed hands many times as the British and French struggled for dominance. The Seven Years' War waged by the two powers for supremacy in North America ended in 1763 with the loss to France of Canada and several Caribbean islands—all ceded to Great Britain by the Treaty of Paris. Not long afterwards, the French reclaimed some islands, most of them only temporarily. The strife grew more intense during the American Revolution, when France sided with American rebels against Great Britain.

In 1782 the British, under Admiral George Rodney, defeated the French in the Battle of the Saints. The next year, in line with the Treaty of Versailles, St. Vincent and Grenada were returned to Great Britain. This time Britannia ruled for nearly two centuries. St. Lucia, however, went to the French.

Owing to the French Revolution and its aftermath, the French were losing their grip on the Caribbean. Under the Treaty of Amiens (1802), Trinidad (captured by the British in 1797) was formally ceded to Great Britain. St. Lucia was transferred to the British in 1814 at the end of the Napoleonic Wars.

Towards Independence

Enlightened thought in France and England condemned slavery and encouraged revolutions, such as the one on Hispaniola in 1791. Toussaint L'Ouverture, a former slave, eventually turned part of that island into the world's first black democracy—a country called Haiti. England outlawed slave-trading in 1807, as did the French in 1818. Slavery itself was abolished in all British colonies in 1833, taking effect the next year. The French followed suit in 1848.

But there was no one to plough the fields. New labour was needed, especially on Trinidad, and tens of thousands of workers were brought to the island from India. The cultural impact was considerable.

Although the early 20th century was an era of self expression and nationalism elsewhere in the Caribbean, the southern islands stayed under the aegis of Great Britain until the 1960s, and most of them did not gain complete independence until the late seventies. The expansion of American influence during and after World War II affected only Trinidad, an oil-refining country of strategic importance, where U.S. bases were constructed.

Attempts have been made at unifying Caribbean government and administration, but the island nations rarely agree. The most they have achieved is a vague cooperative economic community, called Caricom.

While the former British islands are firmly self-governing today, the atmosphere remains British, with parliamentary governments and administrations still based on British models. But each island has its own character and problems. Throughout the Southern Caribbean, governments have discovered that they have a huge economic resource in tourism which continues to grow by leaps and bounds.

Some islands were more farsighted than others, building efficient airports with the help of outside capital and aiding the tourist with a minimum of bureaucracy. On these islands you'll find plenty of new shops and luxury resort hotels. Others remain relatively untouched by the tourist explosion. Those who love the small Southern Caribbean islands fervently hope that future development will not detract from their outstanding natural beauty, nor from the dignity of their people.

WHERE TO GO

All of the islands in the Southern Caribbean lie roughly within 30 minutes to one hour of one another by air. Barbados has a huge modern airport and serves as the main port of entry to the area. In addition, the tourist industry is highly developed, and there's plenty to see and do.

Frequent flights link Barbados to St. Lucia, 160 km (100 miles) to the northwest, and there are also some direct international air connections. Relaxation and friendship with a French flavour highlight a visit to St. Lucia.

Barbadians and tourists alike take to the waters of the soothing Caribbean or the bracing Atlantic.

St. Vincent's blue waters and lush greenery present the perfect starting point for heading out to the other islands.

St. Vincent, 34 km (21 miles) south of St. Lucia, can be reached by plane or boat. The island, a pleasant holiday destination in itself, also makes a logical starting point for downwind yacht tours of the Grenadines. You can also travel by scheduled service between St. Vincent, the idyllic Grenadines, and Grenada—a strikingly beautiful island with exceptional beaches.

Oil-rich Trinidad has remarkable island scenery, though industrial development has taken its toll of the landscape. It is generally easier to travel to Trinidad by jet or small plane, rather than by scheduled boat service. The Carnival season is undoubtedly the most exciting time to visit.

It's usually more satisfactory to fly to the easy-going resort island of Tobago, as the boat journey from Trinidad can be uncomfortable. Good bathing, tranquillity, and scenic beauty bring tourists back to the island year after year.

We cover the islands in counter-clockwise order, starting with Barbados.

BARBADOS

Barbados lies outside the main island chain, about 160 km (100 miles) to the east of St. Vincent in the path of the cooling trade winds. This small, pear-shaped island teems with 253,000 inhabitants—though you're rarely aware of crowds, except on a shopping day in Bridgetown, the capital. Barbados is as British as teatime, not that there isn't plenty of tropical beauty. Pristine Caribbean beaches are edged with palms, and the windswept Atlantic coast with its high cliffs has a rugged appeal.

Unlike the volcanic islands, Barbados is capped by limestone and coral, which means that when rain falls (more than you'd think), it's trapped underground to be drawn in a pure state from wells.

Barbados extends a welcome as warm as the climate, and you'll find the people friendly and genuinely helpful. Accommodation ranges from simple beach cottages to posh resorts that rival the world's best. Everything is geared to help the tourist relax, and you won't find a more comprehensive array of sports facilities anywhere in the Caribbean. Modern music and lively entertainment keep night-owls amused till dawn, and many people from other islands come over to join in the fun.

Roads are acceptable, and you can easily drive yourself around the island. However, it's a good idea to take a semi-private tour or hire a taxi to guide you around at first. Guides and drivers will tell you that Barbados is divided into 11 parishes. The divisions can be confusing at first, but after a few days you'll know that Bridgetown is in St. Michael's, resort development centres around Christ Church, and the Platinum Coast beaches are in St. James's.

Historical Highlights

Barbados maintains closer ties with England than any other Southern Caribbean island. After nearly 350 years of British rule, many Barbadians are ardent Anglophiles. British visitors will detect in their charming hybrid accent something of the Midlands—and a hint of a soft Scottish brogue.

Barbados was sighted by a Portuguese explorer, Pedro a Campos, in 1536. He called the island Los Barbudos ("the bearded ones") after the hoary-looking banyan trees whose hanging roots resembled beards. But Pedro made no claims on Barbados. A century later, in 1625, an English ship touched land at Jamestown, later named Holetown. Once the island had been claimed for England, there were no invasions by rival powers, a record for this part of the world.

Soon Barbados boasted tobacco, cotton, and sugar cane plantations, with stills for the manufacture of rum. Slaves were introduced to work the cane fields, and by 1666 the black population numbered 50,000, compared to 8,000 English slave owners. On Barbados slaves were treated relatively well, and there were no cataclysmic urprisings to compare with other islands to the north, such as Haiti.

Today's white population shares a complex ancestry of former masters and indentured servants, political prisoners, and free-thinkers from Ireland and Scotland—jailbirds who dared to try a bit of crime or even a new religion.

Although politically peaceful throughout the centuries, the island was sporadically ravaged by plague, yellow fever, and hurricanes. Nevertheless, Barbados flourished, especially as an attractive holiday destination. One early tourist, George Washington, paid a visit in 1751 with his half-brother, Lawrence, ill with consumption.

In the 17th and 18th centuries, planters built elegant Great Houses with breezy verandahs overlooking immaculately trimmed gardens. After the abolition of slavery in 1833, Barbados gradually moved towards independence. Its parliament, founded in 1639, is the third oldest in the British

Fishing boats dock after a day in Bridgetown Harbour.

EVINRUDE
65
120

Commonwealth. The island achieved full independence within the Commonwealth in 1966, and became a member of the United Nations. Barbados has been considered one of the most stable island-nations in the Caribbean, perhaps due in part to an exceptionally high literacy rate of 99 percent.

Bridgetown

Today's bustling centre of commerce and seagoing activity was officially founded by the Earl of Carlisle in 1628. The capital probably takes its name from an old Indian bridge that is said to have spanned the River Constitution. Bear in mind that Bridgetown streets can be very hot and crowded about noon; try to visit the town early in the day. Start your tour in **National Heroes Square**, a bustling plaza at the centre of city activity. Taxis and buses usually stop nearby in Broad Street, a colourful thoroughfare with old colonial buildings, including shops packed with duty-free bargains. In the square you'll see a dignified bronze monument to Lord Nelson, erected in honour of the admiral in 1813. Although London's famous memorials may be bigger, Bridgetown's was the first by many years.

Just north of the square, you'll notice the quaint neo-Gothic **Parliament Buildings**, constructed to house the Barbados legislature after a fire in 1860 destroyed most of the neighbourhood. Little streets leading from the Parliament Buildings to Swan Street contain old and new examples of Barbados architecture.

Across Chamberlain Bridge, you'll see the **Carenage**—a shallow inlet where boats were careened (from a French expression for "to turn over") for repair, caulking, and paint-

Barbados, which lies outside the main island chain, is in the path of the cooling trade winds.

ing. Fishing boats and pleasure yachts bob cheerfully in the harbour, alongside replicas of the pirate ships that roamed the Caribbean two centuries ago; they sail again, pressed into service on sightseeing cruises. A submarine, the **Atlantis**, takes tourists a mile out—and 130 feet down—for a close-up look at the reef.

Walk in a northeasterly direction past the bus terminus to **Fairchild Market**, where sellers tempt passers-by with the luscious tropical produce of Barbados and neighbouring islands. The market is at its liveliest early in the morning when fruit and vegetables are at their freshest. From here, take O'Neal Bridge to National Heroes Street and St. Michael's Row, the site of **St. Michael's Cathedral**. This typical Caribbean-style Anglican edifice dates from 1831. The self-appointed guides will tell you more than you want to know about the coral-rock structure with wooden choir stalls and galleries. While Barbados has churches of many denominations, Anglican still predominates.

Up the road from St. Michael's, you come to Queen's Park, an elegant former official residence that housed the British Commanding General until the beginning of this century. Now art exhibitions are held here, and performances are staged in a theatre. The adjacent park boasts an enormous baobab tree that measures over 60 feet in circumference.

To the east lies the **Belleville** district, a residential area full of pretty Victorian houses, and **Government House**, the residence of the Governor General, the representative of the English Crown. The venerable mansion dates from the early 18th century, making it one of the oldest buildings on the island.

Big cruise ships put in at the Deep Water Harbour, situated about a mile from the centre of Bridgetown. A tourist office has been established nearby for the convenience of cruise passengers. Also in the vicinity is the Pelican Crafts

The grand scale of St. John's Church recalls the prosperity of the first half of the 19th century.

Village, established in 1958 to promote local handiwork—worth a short visit.

The **Garrison Savannah**, former British military headquarters, lies on the southern outskirts of town. A race track and playing fields are situated on the old parade grounds, and the military prison now houses the **Barbados Museum**. Don't fail to see this gem of the Caribbean. Scattered about the grassy courtyard are sugar moulds, penny-farthing bicycles, and ships' anchors. Gallery exhibits highlight local lore, seashells, fish, and Arawak culture. There is a special display of prints relating to the islands, as well as fine English furniture. The museum buildings even preserve a neat but dreary prison cell.

Nearby **St. Ann's Fort** dates from the early years of the 18th century. The fortification. with its conspicuous clock tower, has become a local landmark.

Atlantic Sights

The rugged Atlantic coast merits at least a short visit. Take the coast road from Bridgetown to the pleasant resorts of Hastings, St. Lawrence, Maxwell, and Oistins Bay; or travel inland through green sugar cane country, past little churches and tiny towns with gingerbread houses. You may want to visit the Christ Church parish church above Oistins, with its puzzling **"Mystery Vault"**. During the last century, the coffins contained here were said to have changed position, and to this day the mystery has never been solved.

As you approach the southeast, the sea grows more agitated and steep white headlands plunge down to the shore. Admire the windswept and dramatic view from **Crane Beach**, where the sea can be quite rough.

Somewhat farther to the northeast is **Sam Lord's Castle**, a hotel that happens to be a prime tourist attraction. For a small admission fee you can visit the old plantation house, beautifully decorated with furniture of Barbados mahogany made locally in the Regency style. Much of the china and many of the portraits on display were spoils taken from ships wrecked on the rocks offshore by the legendary Sam Lord, who is said to have hung lanterns from the cliffs to lure the ships onto the shallow reef. The house itself looks like a Georgian architectural hybrid, but the site is incomparable.

From here you can head inland to **Oughterson National Wildlife Park**, a nature preserve attractively situated in the grounds of a plantation Great House. This is a good place to see Caribbean birds and animals in their natural habitat.

Among the inhabitants here are lively Barbados monkeys, tropical birds of the most outrageously coloured feathers, fearsome alligators, and more benign but similarly lethargic turtles. The park, officially opened in 1983, also aims to bring children into closer contact with some of the more approachable of the local animals, including rabbits, sheep, and ducks.

There are several points of interest in the St. John's area. **Villa Nova**, a dignified old Great House, has been tastefully refurbished as a luxury hotel. It is still complete with beauti-

Trace the footsteps of the notorious Sam Lord, wrecker of the Barbados coast, by touring his Great House, now a hotel.

Wild orchids are one of the many dozens of flowers that can be found at the Andromeda Gardens.

ful furnishings that enhance the light and airy building, and its gardens and grounds are immaculately kept.

St. John's Church, perched 250 metres (825 feet) above sea level, offers lovely views of the St. John's area. The present structure dates back to 1836, and the cemetery, older still, contains the mossy grave of Ferdinando Paleologus, a possible descendant of the Byzantine emperors.

Now follow the coast road north to picturesque **Bathsheba** (with the accent on the first syllable), where small pastel houses cling gallantly to chalky cliffs that rise high above the raging Atlantic. Holidaying Barbadians flock to the wild and windy Bathsheba region because it is less expensive, less frequented, and cooler than the other shores in summer.

You may want to visit **Andromeda Gardens**, a privately owned botanical garden containing dozens of varieties of flowers, plants, and trees. Among them is the shaggy bearded banyan tree that inspired the name "Barbados."

From Bathsheba the coast road becomes narrow and dangerous in places, but you'll enjoy the view, especially from **The Potteries**, a village of ceramic craftsmen situated on the summit of Chalky Mount at the healthy altitude of 174m (571ft). You can also see the green and rugged hills of the Scotland district, named for its resemblance to its namesake.

In the area is another botanical showplace: the **Flower Forest at Richmond Plantation**. Some splendid views of the sea and Scotland district compete with the horticultural attractions, from ginger lilies to cabbage palms.

Return to Bridgetown via Gun Hill in St. George's parish, the site of a former signal station that communicated messages to St. Ann's Fort. The lion carved out of a rock jutting from the hillside was the work of a British soldier. Nearby, St. George's Church, an 18th-century edifice, preserves an **altarpiece** of the Resurrection from the same century by the American artist Benjamin West.

The Platinum Coast

The west coast takes its name from the brilliant white of its sandy beaches. Many luxury hotels and big private mansions are situated along this "Millionaire's Row." Nevertheless, between the resort developments and imposing estates you can still see wooden Barbadian houses with their gingerbread decoration.

Heading west from Bridgetown, you pass scenic Paradise Beach in St. James's parish. The turquoise water grows clearer and the beaches whiter as you progress towards Payne's Bay and Sandy Lane Bay, a favourite haunt of film personalities as well as English royalty. In Holetown, a monument commemorates the founding of Barbados' first settlement by Englishmen from the ship *Olive Blossom*. However, the date inscribed here, 1625, predates the actual landing by some 20 years. The Anglican **St. James's Church**, founded in 1660 and rebuilt in 1874, preserves a 17th-century font and a large bell inscribed "God Bless King William, 1696."

Drive inland a short distance from Holetown to **Welchman Hall Gully**. This vast tropical forest, now running wild, was originally a spice plantation. You can still see nutmeg, cinnamon, and fruit trees among the lush lianas and parasite vines. The walk through the grounds can take a good half hour or so, even at a brisk clip. Nearby is **Harrison's Cave**, where a special tram will take you down through an exciting cavern of stalactites and stalagmites.

Return to the coast and travel north again to **Speightstown** (pronounced "spite"), once the sugar capital of the northwest area. The town was known as "Little Bristol," since the Speight family did most of their trade with the English port. Speightstown has remained typically West Indian, with small, pastel wooden houses and shops, old churches, and an easy-going populace greeting one another in the streets. Just north at Six Men's Bay, old cannon are ranged about the silvery shore, another picturesque reminder of the past.

Continue north through flat sugar cane country to North Point and **Animal Flower Cave**, where a willing guide will lead you down steep steps to a cavern carved out by the sea. You'll see the animal flower itself—an exquisite, tentacled sea anemone that recoils when you touch it. Bring rubber-soled shoes. Before you go, check with the tourist office in case high waves have caused the closing of the cave.

On the return journey, take the road that winds through St. Lucy's parish to Cherry Tree Hill, 259 metres (850 feet)

Barbados Briefing

Airport. Grantley Adams International Airport is the most modern and efficient airport in the Southern Caribbean area, with bank, restaurant, bar, tourist information service, car-hire agencies, public telephones, several duty-free shops, and postal facilities. It is completely air-conditioned. The airport is about 13 km (18 miles) from the capital. Bus service is inexpensive, and some hotels fetch guests in mini-buses. On leaving Barbados, visitors must pay a departure tax.

Currency. Barbados dollar (BD$), 100 cents = BD$1. Issued in 2, 5, 10, 20, 50, and 100-dollar notes, and coins of l, 5, 10, and 25 cents and 1 dollar.

Electric Current. 110 volts, 50 cycle AC. Various plug systems are in use, from American to British.

Emergencies. Dial 211 for police, 311 for fire, 511 for ambulance.

Hospital. Queen Elizabeth General Hospital, St Michael, tel.436-6450; Bay View hospital, tel: 436-5446.

Hours. Business and shopping hours are generally 8 a.m. to 4-5 p.m. weekdays. On Saturday shops open from 8 a.m. to noon. Banks: Monday to Thursday 8 a. m. to 3 p.m., Friday 8 a. m. to 5 p.m. or 8 a.m. to l p.m. and 3 to 5p.m.

Newspapers. The *Barbados Advocate* and the *Nation* publish daily; magazines for tourists include the *Visitor* and the *Sun Seeker.*

Public Holidays. New Year's Day (January 1), Errol Barrow's Day (January 21), Good Friday and Easter Monday (movable), Labor Day (May 1), Whit Monday (movable), Kadooment Day (first Monday day in August), United Nations Day (first Monday in October), Independence Day (November 30), Christmas Day and Boxing Day (December 25 and 26).

Tourist Information Offices

Barbados: Barbados Board of Tourism, Harbour Road, P. O. Box 242, Bridgetown, tel. 427-2623, and at the airport

Canada: Barbados Board of Tourism, 105 Adelaide Street West, Suite 1010, Toronto, Ontario M5H 1P9, tel. (416) 214-9880

U. K.: Barbados Board of Tourism, 263 Tottenham Court Road, London W1T 7LA, tel. (020) 7636-9448

U. S. A.: Barbados Board of Tourism, 800 Second Avenue, New York NY 10017, tel. (212) 986-6516/8; also BTA offices in Florida and California.

Oblique view of a venerable relic: the old Morgan Lewis windmill recalls days when sugar was king of the islands.

high. There are no cherry trees in sight, only mahogany, the robust tree that was first planted on the island in 1763.

Farley Hill, once a venerable plantation house, lies a short distance away over a road with many turns. Many royal visitors were entertained here, including King George V, and the house was the setting for the film *Island in the Sun*. Today Farley Hill is little more than a ruin. Take a walk over the green lawns and admire the view of the Scotland district.

Opposite the entrance to Farley Hill, the **Barbados Wildlife Preserve** is home to the Barbados descendant of the African green monkey.

Nicholas Abbey, another plantation house in the area, delights visitors with its Persian arches and well-kept gardens. A short distance east stands the **Morgan Lewis Windmill**, a well-restored reminder of the days when sugar-making was introduced by Dutch settlers from Brazil. They soon left sugar cultivation to the British, however. To return to Bridgetown, take Highway 2A, an inland route that is also the most direct.

ST. LUCIA

This beautiful volcanic island midway between Martinique and St. Vincent has some of the best scenery in the Caribbean: rugged jungle, undulating agricultural land, dazzling beaches, and the volcanic, cone-shaped Pitons. There's even a dormant but still-bubbling volcano called Soufrière that can be viewed from inside without danger.

Francophiles love St. Lucia for its French atmosphere. Many place-names are French, from the capital, Castries, to Vieux Fort on the southern tip of the island. English is the official language, but most of the 140,000 inhabitants also speak French patois, a reminder of the French colonization.

While St. Lucia (pronounced LOO-sha) remains agricultural, with bananas the most significant crop, tourism is rapidly developing as an important revenue earner. You can be very comfortable here, and there are provisions for all sorts of summer sports. Enjoy good music every night and indulge in the excellent native cuisine, with its coconuts, bananas, and tropical spices.

Typical West Indian cottage, Santa Lucia

Idyllic days on the tranquil waters of Marigot Bay in St. Lucia — ideal for mooring and perfect for a swim.

Historical Highlights

Carib Indians had St. Lucia more or less to themselves until the early 17th century, when a group of Englishmen from the ship *Olive Blossom* landed and tried to set up a colony. Within a span of weeks, however, the Caribs had killed most of them. Again, in 1639, there was an abortive 18-month attempt by some Englishmen to colonize the island, but they, too, were driven off by the Caribs.

The French were eyeing beautiful and strategically placed St. Lucia as well; so began a tug-of-war history in which St. Lucia was constantly changing hands. In all, St. Lucia bounced between British and French control 13 times before being ceded to Britain in 1814 by the Treaty of Paris.

In 1765, during one brief French reign, the first sugar plantation was started and small towns were built up. But trouble began as the American and French revolutions spread to the West Indies. The 19th century—an era of coconut, sugar cane, coffee, and cotton plantations—was largely a peaceful time. Emancipation was met with ecstasy by the former slaves.

In 1967 St. Lucia became an Associated State of Britain with full internal self-government and was granted political independence on February 22, 1979. After a period of mild instability caused by a tug-of-war between the leadership of two political parties, the island returned to its usual state of calm.

Castries

The capital was named in 1785 after the Maréchal de Castries, then Minister of Marine responsible for the French colonies. However, few buildings remain from the 18th century, mainly due to two devastating fires that swept the town in 1948 and 1951. Today's city of about 60,000 inhabitants looks frankly jerry-built, though some quarters have a certain charm.

Take a look at the scenic **yacht basin** and the ultramodern **Pointe Seraphine** duty-free shopping complex at the harbour, including entertainment and restaurants. It caters to all kinds of tourists, not just cruise-ship passengers. In the busy Castries market, you'll see plenty of island produce for sale, the array varying with the season.

Along Bridge Street, you'll find the central post office and the largest shops. Spacious **Derek Walcott Square**, one of the capital's few picturesque corners, boasts tropical greenery, with shade provided by a samman tree and a huge mahogany. The 19th-century Catholic cathedral has interesting wooden columns, iron vaulting, and frescoes painted by a pupil of the French artist Puvis de Chavannes. Opposite the cathedral stands the most handsome building in town, the Central Library. This red-and-white structure of stucco and

The faithful of Castries pray in their ornate cathedral.

stone, named officially after its benefactors, the Carnegies of America, looks older than it is (19th century).

Castries may lack charm but the capital is backed up by its own mountain, Morne Fortune, which means "Lucky Hill." A drive to the top up precipitous roads leads to 18th-century **Fort Charlotte**, an unremarkable military installation with good views. Both French and British conducted their squabbles from the ramparts.

In the middle of the 19th century, three other military buildings were erected on Morne Fortune. The buildings have been restored and now form part of the island's principal educational complex. But you can still see many reminders of the British and French forces who fought each other for St. Lucia. From this hill you also have a sweeping view of Castries harbour, Vigie peninsula, Pigeon Island, and the Pitons.

Towards the North

Many of the island's luxury hotels are situated to the north of Castries along a road as good as it is scenic. The hotels are friendly places and they admit non-residents for drinks, meals, or a swim. In the area are sparkling crescent-shaped beaches, such as Vigie Beach, Choc Beach, and Gros Islet.

A causeway links **Pigeon Island** to the mainland. The islet, remarkable for its high, green hill, finds favour with energetic climbers. Bring a picnic lunch and settle down for a while to enjoy the beautiful views of Martinique to the north. The island was the main base of Admiral Rodney in the 18th century, and the name "pigeon" probably comes from Rodney's hobby of breeding the birds. Today the abandoned stone barracks once used by the British garrison looks like a haunted villa. The barracks, together with a museum, is situated within the national park that has been developed on Pigeon Point.

North of Pigeon Island, scenery turns rocky and weather breezy, but the cool, green hill region has attracted entrepreneurs. Land in Cap Estate is being snapped up and the northern area has sprouted a marina, golf course, shops, hotel, and residential development at Rodney Bay.

Exploring the South

Soufrière volcano and the Pitons are not to be missed on any visit to St. Lucia. You can reach these spectacular sights by boat on a pleasant day's cruise, by organized tour, or by car. It's wise to hire a driver familiar with all the hair-raising bends. The circular coastal road that travels around the southern two-thirds of the island was established in the 18th century by the Maréchal de Laborie.

Just south of Castries, you pass Cul de Sac, an aptly named sheltered harbour lined with banana plants—bananas being St.

Lucia's biggest agricultural product. Next comes Marigot Bay, a secluded and idyllic palm-fringed spot with several hotels and restaurants. Farther along are more attractive and isolated bays and beaches: Anse la Raye, where local people make boats from gum trees and sails from flour bags, Anse Cochon (French for "pig"), and the little fishing village of Canaries.

By land or by sea, the sight of the cone-shaped **Pitons** will take your breath away. Postcards give no more than an idea of the majestic beauty of these volcanic mountains—the Gros Piton (798 metres/2,619 feet) and the Petit Piton (790 metres/2,460 feet).

Soufrière town, typically West Indian with brightly painted arcaded buildings, nestles just under the twin mountains. Unspoiled as the town looks, the locals have seen all too many tour groups. Although official guides and the police formally discourage begging, you may be assailed by self-styled guides, palms extended for money, or little boys who forget school to dive naked for coins.

Local Patois

On St. Lucia everybody speaks English and most people understand French. But among themselves, islanders converse in patois, a dialect based on French. However, the syntax differs from French, genders are often dropped, and the letter "r" sounds more like "w." Negatives are made by putting "pa" (like the French pas) before a verb. Needless to say, only a practiced ear can understand it.

It is not mine.	Sé pa sa-mwe. *Say pa sam-wehng*
How much is it?	Kome i kuté? *Kong mehng eekoo-tay*
What a pretty place.	Mi yõ bel coté. *Mee yong behl ko-tay*

Don't miss the spectacular cones of the Pitons, the volcanic mountains near Soufrière town.

Follow the road leading to the renovated **sulphur baths**, situated just outside town. The baths were discovered by the French, and in 1784 Maréchal de Laborie, then in command of the island, sent samples of the water to Paris. They were analyzed by Louis XVI's doctors, who pronounced the source to be beneficial. The water gurgles and steams in a jungle setting of dense vegetation. It's a picturesque sight, you're welcome to take a dip.

A path leads through the tropical forest to the source. Don't plunge your hand into the water; it is boiling hot and can burn. If you walk farther along the path, beyond the hottest part of the source, you come to a lovely waterfall and pond. Do not wade or bathe here. This is a known breeding ground for the highly dangerous bilharzia parasite.

From the baths, take the twisting road to **Soufrière**, advertised as the world's only drive-in volcano. The road goes right up to the crater, steaming away like an inferno. Competent guides lead you on foot quickly over the hot stones and through the noxious sulphur gases to an untouchable black pit where the steaming water reaches 100°C (212°F). Efforts are being made to harness the steam energy for geothermal use. Note that some rocks are coloured green by copper deposits, white by lime, and chalk and yellow by sulphur.

Again take the road south and make for Choiseul and Laborie, two ramshackle but picturesque little villages surrounded by splendid vegetation. You'll see men with machetes harvesting crops of bananas, cocoa, citrus fruit, coconuts, peanuts, sweet potatoes, or cabbage, depending on the season.

The road levels out as it reaches Vieux Fort and Hewanorra, the island's international airport. The name has its origin in a Carib word meaning "Land of the Iguana." Iguanas, large lizards that are harmless unless attacked, have dwindled in number on the island. You're unlikely to see one, unless you climb a mountain or stay at one of the hotels that keep a pet iguana in a cage.

A picturesque lighthouse stands on Moule a Chique cape. On a clear day the view from the cape is spectacular. If you look out to sea, you'll glimpse the island of St. Vincent. Look inland, across St. Lucia, and you'll see the Pitons. The seemingly endless Atlantic beach that stretches north of the cape is well whipped by winds and decorated with a glossy hotel.

As you travel up the east coast, you'll find the circular road somewhat easier going, not that there isn't plenty to keep a driver alert—whether children on their way home from school or cows, donkeys, and sheep wandering on the road. Headlands project into the ocean, and there are two little towns to explore, Micoud and Dennery. Inland, midway between them, rises Mt. Gimie, at 950 metres (3,117 feet) the highest point on the island.

St. Lucia Briefing

Airports. St. Lucia has two airports. Hewanorra Airport, the larger of the two, is at the southern end of the island (about 60km (38 miles) from the capital and most hotels). The airport has small duty-free shops, car hire agencies, and a tourist information office but is not air conditioned. There is an air link to the other airport, George Charles Airport, conveniently situated near most of the better hotels and Castries. Customs is informal, and there is usually someone from the tourist office on hand, as well as a car-hire agency representative. Small planes from Hewanorra and the other islands land here. Both airports levy a departure tax.

Currency. Eastern Caribbean dollar (EC$), 100 cents=EC$1. Notes: EC$ 1, 5, 20, and 100. Coins: 1, 2, 5, 10, 25, 50 cents, and EC$1.

Electric Current. 220/240 volts, 50 cycle AC. Some hotels have 110 volt outlets in rooms. The British 3-prong plug system is in use.

Emergencies. Dial 911 for police, ambulance, or fire.

Hospitals: Victoria Hospital, Castries, tel. 452 2421. St. Jude's Hospital, Vieux Fort, tel. 454 6041

Hours. Business and shopping: 8 a.m. to 12:30 p.m. and 1:30 to 4 p.m. Monday to Friday, Saturday 8 a.m. to noon. Banking hours: 8 a. m. to 3 p. m. Monday to Thursday, Friday 8 a. m. to noon and 3 to 5 p. m.

Public Holidays. New Year's Day (January 1), Independence Day (22 Feb), Good Friday and Easter Monday (March/April), Labour Day (1 May), Whit Monday (May/June), Corpus Christi (June), Emancipation Day (August 7), Thanksgiving Day (October), National Day (December 13th), Christmas Day and Boxing Day (December 25 and 26).

Tourist Information Offices

St. Lucia: St. Lucia Tourist Board, Point Seraphine, Castries, tel. 452 4094

Canada: St. Lucia Tourist Board, 8 King Street East, Suite 700, Toronto, Ontario; tel. (416) 862-4242

U K: St. Lucia Tourist Board, 421A, Finchley Road, London NW3 6HJ, tel. (020) 7431 3675

U S.A.: St. Lucia Tourist Board, 9th Floor, 820 Second Avenue, New York, NY 10017, tel. (212) 867-2950

Dennery earned renown as a den of iniquity, and until the 1950s a part of town called Oléon (or Aux Lyons) was closed to outsiders. Townspeople made a strong (and illegal) local brew known as *mal cochon,* and they were so belligerent in the defense of their privacy that even the police were reluctant to interfere.

Roads don't travel inland on St. Lucia, but guides can lead you over the hills and through the jungle if you're willing to hike. Although a few deadly *fer-de-lance* snakes inhabit the tropical forest, you're unlikely to see one; and the trip is worthwhile for the animal and bird life you encounter, including the colourful, blue-headed St. Lucia parrot.

From Dennery the circular road winds gradually back across the island in the direction of La Toc and Castries. To

Soufrière is known for the world's only drive-through volcano, with a road leading right up to the crater.

reach the capital, you cross through the flat Cul de Sac plantation and up a mountain road with good sea views.

ST. VINCENT AND THE GRENADINES

Constant and intense volcanic activity through the ages has endowed St. Vincent with a fringe of shiny black-sand beaches, notably on the Atlantic side. Bleakly spectacular, they contrast with the lush terraced hills inland. The island's 344 square km (133 square miles) form a rough ellipse with a bump on the western side. Soufrière volcano bubbles out of the narrower northern end, and, unlike St. Lucia's, this one still erupts. During periods of volcanic activity, ash has been spewed as far as Barbados, 160 km (100 miles) to the east.

Aside from problems caused by volcanic eruptions, nature has been kind to St. Vincent's 107,000 inhabitants. Bananas, coconuts, cacao, eddoes, and yams all flourish on the "Breadfruit Island," so called because it was the first in the Caribbean to be planted with the bumpy-skinned vegetable brought to the islands from the South Pacific by the legendary Captain Bligh. The island has long been the world's greatest producer of arrowroot, a starch used in the preparation of baby food and cooking sauces. Sea-island cotton, one of the softest fibres in the world, is still exported, although not in great quantity anymore.

Historical Highlights

Like neighbouring islands, St. Vincent passed back and forth between the British and French, especially during the troubled 18th century, when the whole Caribbean area was in turmoil. European supremacy was never absolute, for the Caribs fought with all their mettle and ferocity. Several times the French seemed to make progress with the tribe, and they attempted to teach them the elements of trade.

Towards the end of the 17th century, a boatload of African slaves was shipwrecked on the Atlantic shore. The Caribs welcomed them, and soon a new race of Black Caribs sprang up. (A few descendants of this mixing still inhabit St. Vincent today.)

But the Caribs remained basically hostile, and they often rose against the Europeans. In 1748 St. Vincent was declared a kind of no-man's-land by both British and French, who were at their wits' end with belligerent Amerindians. The island was officially ceded to the British in 1763, only to be taken by the French in 1779, then made British in 1783.

In 1795 islanders sided with the French against British colonizers in the Brigands' War—murdering, burning down houses, and setting fire to cane fields. However, British reinforcements proved stronger in the end, and in 1796 the British overpowered the opposition and dispatched more than 5,000 troublemakers to Honduras.

Emancipation took place peacefully under British rule. A few years later, indentured labourers were brought from Portugal and India to work the cane fields. To this day, traces of their cultures remain, though many of the original 19th-century workers returned to their homelands.

In 1969 St. Vincent became a British Associated State with internal self-government. Ten years later it achieved complete independence.

On Good Friday, the 13th of April, 1979, the Soufrière volcano blew its top. Other recent disasters, especially a couple of hurricanes, have jolted island agriculture. But tourism has always bounced back.

Kingstown

There are arcades to spare in St. Vincent's unassuming capital, many of them left over from French colonial times. The

On market Saturdays, the people of Kingstown stock up on sturdy baskets, breadfruit, and other fresh produce.

harbour, within sight of Mount St. Andrew and Dorsetshire Hill, is always alive with schooners, fishing boats, and the business of loading island produce. Kingstown's food **market** ranks among the best in the Caribbean, especially on weekend mornings, but the small city offers little else in the way of tourist attractions.

Shops are situated near the seaport and market. In Grenville Street, towards the other end of town, you'll see a trio of churches: St. George's Anglican Cathedral, the Methodist Church, and St. Mary's Roman Catholic Church. This last, a fanciful potpourri of Romanesque, Gothic, and Renaissance styles, would delight any storybook illustrator. There are towers, crosses, and fretwork all over, and courtyards are situated in odd places. Surprisingly, it's a recent construction, built in the 1930s by Benedictine monks from Trinidad.

Learn all about Caribbean plant life at the **Botanic Gardens**, just below the Governor's Residence. The gardens, said to be the oldest in the Western hemisphere, were founded in 1765. Self-appointed guides are more than willing to point out the highlights of the well-maintained site.

Fort Charlotte, just west of Kingstown, merits a visit for the view, if for nothing else. Take a panoramic look at the capital, harbour, and nearby Grenadines through the handy telescope erected at the top of the fort's 194 metres (636 feet). The fort was built by the British as a defense against the French and named after the wife of King George III. Three of the original cannon are still in place, and the look-out point 44 is used for monitoring ships.

The fort saw no military action, unless you count the murder of a Royal Scots sentry in 1824 by a member of his own regiment. The austere former barracks building now serves as a museum displaying colourful contemporary paintings

A snorkel and mask open up an exotic new underwater world.

by William Linze Prescott. The canvases depict some rather lurid scenes from St. Vincent's history.

The Women's Prison, a short distance downhill, looks out on one of the loveliest views in the world. For more stunning views of Kingstown and the harbour, climb east of the city up to **Dorsetshire Hill**, taking the twisting road from Sion Hill near E.T. Joshua airport.

Along the Caribbean Coast

From Kingstown, drive northwest via the Leeward Highway, the name for the narrow road that twists its way along the coast. As you travel northwards, you come upon one stunning sea view after another, and in between there are small towns such as Questelles, a community of primitive houses and neat churches. Just before the small fishing village of Layou Bay, stop to admire **Indian petroglyphs**, stone carvings estimated to be at least 1,400 years old. From here, you can make a short detour inland to the picturesque and jungle-like Vermont district.

Another 5 km (3 miles) brings you to **Barrouallié**, one of the last whaling villages in this part of the world. These days a catch is rare, and you're not very likely to see a whale.

The road winds north again through little settlements with amusing English or French names. One Gallic-named bay, for example, is called Petit Bordel, which means either "Little Brothel" or "Little Mess" in French. Some 48 km (30 miles) from Kingstown, the road comes to an abrupt end near Richmond Beach, a deserted place ideal for a picnic or swim.

Towards the Atlantic

Driving southeast along the coast past the Kingstown airport, you travel through the town's main residential and hotel district into suburbs where English-style mowed lawns surround large villas. You soon see **Young Island**, just 183 metres (200 yards) offshore. Although the island has been developed as a luxury resort, non-residents are able to cross over on the hotel boat to enjoy a drink or a meal and explore the grounds. For a small charge, you'll be permitted to use the pool or the small beach. Fort Duvernette, on an adjacent islet reputed to have figured in battles with the Caribs, is now the scene of torch-lit barbecue suppers.

Head back to the mainland and continue north past a yachting centre and a few good beaches. You enter farming country, including land broken up into small plots planted with peanuts, yams, potatoes, cassava, and corn. Coconuts are another important crop in this fertile area.

The road, now known as the Windward Highway, parallels the shimmering volcanic black-sand beaches of the Atlantic coast. Stop at **Mount Pleasant** for an impressive view of the pounding surf—but beware: winds, rough water, and sharp rocks make swimming in the Atlantic dangerous. Farther along, the green Argyle district, a former plantation still planted with arrowroot, coconuts, and other crops, extends up to Peruvian Vale.

From here to the village of Georgetown you drive through more impressive Atlantic scenery. From Georgetown, a poor road leads to Rabacca Dry River, a region marked by former volcanic activity. You'll need a jeep to continue on to Fancy, a village situated at the northern tip of the island.

Alternatively, you can head inland to the **Mesopotamia** district, otherwise known as the Marriaqua Valley, one of the island's most picturesque regions. **Belvedere Point** looks out over this agricultural area. Green and richly cultivated

Take an afternoon to walk through a Caribbean Eden — St. Vincent's Botanical Gardens, founded in 1765.

A vivid dash of blue provides a striking contrast to the green surroundings on St. Vincent.

fields climb neatly terraced hillsides interspersed with pretty villages. Every inch is planted with peanuts, nutmeg, bananas, and plantain.

There are dizzying drops down to rushing streams and rivers like the Yambou. Every day seems to be laundry day, and you see many women (men, too) beating clothes against stones in the clear rivers. The people are attractive, but very proud. You'll probably annoy them if you brandish a camera. To return to Kingstown, take the Vigie Highway, the most direct road.

La Soufrière

This full day's excursion for the very hardy is best attempted on an organized tour. Starting out early in the morning, you travel by car, switching to a land-rover which carries you over dirt roads to the vicinity of the 1,234-metre (4,048-foot) crater. The climb up takes 2 to 3 hours—through hot (and sometimes rainy) jungle territory, but with plenty of rewarding plant and bird life to be seen.

Soufrière has been well chronicled in recent history as a fairly violent volcano. The biggest explosion occurred in May, 1902, when at least 2,000 inhabitants were killed. Later in the 20th century, a scenic crater lake was formed, and in 1970 and 1971 minor explosions gave birth to an island in the centre of the crater. But all this scenery was destroyed by the gas-and-ash eruption of April 1979. It was not a major disaster, however, since nobody was hurt. Problems came mainly from the big layer of ash that settled down on agricultural growth and temporarily blanketed even the best hotel lobbies.

If you climb to the top of the crater today, you'll find a steaming volcanic dome and pools of water in place of the island and lake. Though walking is arduous, the excursion shouldn't be dangerous, as the volcano is constantly being monitored and warnings are issued when violent activity is foreseen.

Grenadine Highlights

At least 100 islands (600 if you count all the rocky outcrops) extend for some 56 km (35 miles) between St. Vincent and Grenada, like the beads on a necklace. The main islands in St. Vincent's domain—Bequia, Mustique, Canouan, Mayreau, the Tobago Cays, Union, Palm, and Petit St. Vincent—are considered the ultimate Caribbean paradise for fishermen, snorkellers, and yachtsmen. For city dwellers seeking solitude, tranquillity, and extraordinary beauty, there are few island groups that compare with the sparsely populated Grenadines, peopled by fewer than 10,000 inhabitants.

Bequia (BECK-way or BECK-wee). This small but civilized gem about 15 km (9 miles) from St. Vincent has a tiny airport, or you can make the one- to two-hour journey by boat. You dock in Port Elizabeth's colourful **Admiralty Bay**, which is jam-packed with yachts and looks like a festive regatta all year round. On the beach, fishermen mend their nets and make hand-built boats, an important local industry.

Make a visit to the Tourist Board—the small building on the left as you face **Port Elizabeth** from the beach—to orient yourself and plan your stay. The main island sights can be reached in a hired taxi. Allow half a day to see them all. An airstrip has been built near Paget Farm, once a quaint whaling village; roads and hotels are being upgraded and new restaurants opened.

Bequia sights include Old Fort which affords a good view of Admiralty Bay; Vista Point with views of St. Vincent and other islands, Friendship Bay with a couple of hotels; and Moon Hole, a troglodytic residential development that has literally been carved from the cliffs. The road to **Princess Margaret Bay** (noted for its beautiful coral reef, snorkeling, and tranquillity) is poor, but inexpensive water taxis are available from Port Elizabeth.

Mustique (mus-TEEK). The blinding white-sand beaches and undulating green scenery made Mustique a favourite hideaway of Princess Margaret and many other celebrities. But for all its publicity, Mustique looks more like a desert island than a gathering-place for the jet-set.

You may go no farther than one of the sandy beaches or the minuscule port of **Britannia Bay**, a famous yachtsmen's and sailors' haunt—unless you stay at the **Cotton House**, the island's single hotel, a restored 18th-century landmark. This exceedingly luxurious establishment bears all the earmarks of rustic elegance, with louvered windows, Spanish silver screens, and a fountain made from scallop shells.

Canouan. Blessed with beaches that are exceptional, even by Caribbean standards, the island is currently being developed as a discreet resort.

St. Vincent/Grenadines Briefing

Airport. E.T Joshua Airport on St. Vincent accommodates small planes only. The airport has a tourist information counter, bank, bar and restaurant, and two duty-free shops. It is 5-8 km (3-5 miles) from the major hotels, or 5 km (3 miles) to the centre of Kingstown. You could take the colourfully painted bus, but a taxi is faster. The airport charges a small departure tax. For information on getting to the Grenadines, see Inter-Island Travel on page120.

Currency. Eastern Caribbean dollar (EC$), 100 cents = EC$1. You might hear the old term "Bee Wee dollar" (for British West Indies). Notes: EC$ 1, 5, 20, and 100. Coins: 1, 2, 5, 10, 25, 50 cents, and EC$1.

Electric Current. 220/240 volts, 50 cycle AC. U. S. appliances will need a converter.

Emergencies. Dial 99 for police or fire, 61185 for ambulance.

Hospitals. Kingstown has a government hospital, tel. 61185, and a privately owned one, tel. 71747. There are also hospitals in Georgetown and on Bequia (Grenadines).

Hours. General business and shopping hours: Monday to Friday 8 a.m. to noon and 1 to 4 p.m., Saturday 8 a.m. to noon. Banks: Monday to Thursday 8 a.m. to noon or 1 p.m., Friday 8 a.m. to noon or 1 p.m. and 2 or 3 to 5 p.m.

Newspapers. The *News* is published weekly; *The Herald* is a daily paper.

Public Holidays. New Year's Day (January 1), National Heroes' Day (March), Good Friday and Easter Monday (movable), May Day (first Monday in May), Whit Monday (movable), Caribbean Community Day (first Monday in July), Carnival (first Monday and Tuesday in July), Emancipation Day (first Monday in August), Independence Day (last Monday in October), Christmas Day and Boxing Day (December 25 and 26).

Tourist Information Offices

St. Vincent: St. Vincent Tourist Board, Bay Street, Kingstown, tel. (784) 457 1502

U.K.: St. Vincent Tourist Board, 10 Kensington Court, London W8 5DL, tel. (020) 7937-6570

U.S.A.: St. Vincent Tourist Board, 801 Second Avenue, New York, NY 10017, tel. (212) 687-4981

Union and surrounding islands. You can fly to the beautifully mountainous Union, the southernmost of St. Vincent's Grenadines. There are a few small hotels and many beaches. On the resort hotel islands of **Petit St. Vincent** and **Palm Island** life is casual but chic. You can hire small boats for day excursions to islands such as Mayreau and the uninhabited Tobago Cays, where you'll picnic and swim in splendid isolation.

GRENADA

This volcanic island possesses the same kind of rugged beauty that graces St. Vincent and St. Lucia—with one notable difference. Nutmeg, introduced in 1843, has become the island's principal export. In fact, Grenada produces about 25 per cent of the world's supply. It may be the power of suggestion, but the breezes wafting over the "Isle of Spice" do seem aromatic.

There is no shortage of sophisticated hotels and luxury developments on Grenada, and the sandy beaches, including the famed Grand Anse, run on for miles. An organized tour or drive around the island, returning from the east coast by the spectacular inland road, will provide as scenic a tour as you'll find anywhere. You travel through tropical rain forests, past gorges of stunning beauty, and within hailing distance of a dormant volcano. At the end of the trip you return to views of St. George's harbour and the sea—a sun-washed spectacle that incites painters to pick up brush and palette.

Historical Highlights

Columbus sailed past the northern tip of Grenada, now the small port of Levera Bay, which he called Concepción. Spanish sailors later named the island after their native Granada. The French then turned this into Grenada, though the British had the last word, pronouncing it gre-NAY-da.

Columbus was lucky not to have seen the island's beauties too closely, because the Caribs were particularly fierce on Grenada. Early attempts by both British and French to subdue them failed. In 1650, the French under Du Parquet and Le Comte purchased land from the Caribs in exchange for knives and hatchets, brandy and glass beads. But the Caribs weren't pacified for long, and they soon rebelled against the occupiers. A campaign of extermination was carried out. When defeat was certain, the last small group of fighting Caribs jumped to their death from a northern cliff, now known as Morne du Sauteurs, or Leapers' Hill.

The Isle of Spice boasts a wealth of fresh fruits.

By 1705 the French had established a settlement at Fort George, overlooking St. George's harbour. But by 1762 the British had moved in again, ousting the French, who retaliated and regained the island in 1779. This uneasy French rule lasted until the 1783 Treaty of Versailles definitively established British rule, bringing to a close the French-English tug-of-war.

The century closed with a slave uprising in which the Lieutenant-Governor and many British citizens were killed. However, the island settled down after emancipation. It was formally declared a Crown Colony in 1877.

After the establishment of an elected legislature in 1924, Grenada gradually moved towards independence. The island was made a British Associated State in 1967, and became fully independent in 1974. A coup in the spring of 1979 brought several years of unrest, culminating in military intervention by the United States government in October 1983. But things quickly returned to normal, and the tourist industry is booming again.

St. George's

Start your visit to the capital with a stop for maps and information at the Grenada tourist office, situated on the east side of the **Carenage**. The picturesque inner harbour preserves some attractive 18th-century warehouses, and the lively restaurants and bars in the waterfront area make favourite meeting-places for tourists and yachtsmen alike. From here, walk east a short distance to the **Botanical Gardens and Zoo**, majestically heralded by a clump of royal palms. The gardens bloom with an array of tropical flowers, and you may sight some brilliantly plumed Caribbean birds.

Make your way back to the waterside. You'll see Fort George high on its hill, an impressive structure erected by the French in 1705. The building now serves as police headquarters and cannot be visited. Sendall Tunnel leads from the Carenage to the **Outer Harbour** and quayside **Melville Street**, a lively shopping centre. Walk one street inland along Granby Street, a crossroad lined with cosy shops, to **Market Square**, site of a wonderful, typically West Indian open-air market. Among the wares for sale in the area are all manner of straw goods, carvings, and paintings. The profusion of local spices— from nutmeg to ginger root —will find favour with the most demanding gourmet.

Follow Granby Street to the crossroads with Church Street, named after the churches that line it. Pay particular

Grenada/Grenadines-Briefing

Airports. Grenada's Point Salines International Airport, situated at Point Saline, 6 km (4 miles) south of the capital and approximately 3 km (2 miles) from the main hotel area, has direct service to and from the U.S. There is a taxi service. For information on getting to Carriacou and Petit Martinique, see Inter Island Travel, pages 118–119.

Currency. Eastern Caribbean dollar (EC$) 100 cents = EC$1. Also referred to as "Bee Wee" (British West indian) currency. Notes: EC$ l, 5, 20, and 100. Coins: l, 2, 5, 10, 25, 50 cents, and EC$1.

Electric Current. 220/240 volts, 50 cycle AC.

Emergencies. Dial 911 for police or fire, 434 for ambulance (St. George's).

Hospitals. General Hospital, St. George's, tel. 440 2051. Also Princess Alice Hospital in St. Andrew's parish, tel. 442 7251.

Hours. General business and shopping: Monday to Friday 8 a.m. to 4 p.m. A few shops and offices close for lunch (about 11:45 a.m. to 1 p.m.). Thursday and Saturday 8 a.m. to noon only. Banking hours: Monday to Thursday 8 a.m. to noon, Friday 8 a.m. to noon and 2:30 to 4:30 p.m.

Newspapers. The *Grenadian Voice* and *Informer.* (dailies); *Grenada Today* (weekly).

Public Holidays. New Year's Day (January 1), Independence Day (February 7), Good Friday and Easter Monday (movable), Labour Day (May 1), Whit Monday (movable), Corpus Christi (movable), Emancipation Day (first Monday in August), Carnival (August), Christmas Day and Boxing Day (December 25 and 26).

Tourist Information Offices

Grenada: Grenada Board of Tourism, P.O. Box 293, The Carenage, St. George's, tel. 440 2001

Canada: Grenada Tourist Office, Suite 820, 439 University Avenue, Toronto, Ontario M5G lY8, tel. (416) 595-1343

U.K.: Grenada Tourist Board, 1 Collingham Gardens, Earls Court, London SW5 OHW, tel. (020) 7370-5164

U.S.A.: Grenada Tourism Office, 800 Second Avenue, Suite 900D, New York, NY 10017, tel. (212) 587-9554

The inner harbour of St. George — one of the most striking sights in the Southern Caribbean.

attention to the **clock tower** of the Anglican church, which has become something of a town symbol, and note, too, the tower of the Presbyterian kirk. Return to Granby and take its continuation (Lucas Street) all the way up to Richmond Hill and Fort Frederick, a magnificent lookout point. Construction was begun by the French in 1779, but it was the British who applied the finishing touches in 1783.

The residence of the Governor General nearby is known as "Government House," but the building is distinguished only for the views it affords.

Points South

Head south from St. George's along the **Royal Drive**, named in honour of Queen Elizabeth II, who was escorted this way on a tour of the island (allow two hours for the complete circuit). You'll probably want to stop on the Morne Jaloux Ridge to admire views fit for a queen.

The road winds down through green hills past neat, small settlements, and farming country to Westerhall Point, a landscaped residential area which grows greener and wilder towards the point that projects into the sea. As you reach Point Jeudy, you'll see black volcanic rock rearing out of an active sea.

Continue to Woburn, a quiet little fishing village, then on to Lance aux Epines and Prickly Point, site of a few hotels and a bathing beach. From here, the road travels through the cane fields of Woodlands, which has a sugar factory. Along the route there are good views of pretty little coves. At Point Saline you pass the international airport.

Caribbean and Atlantic waters come together here, and the black, volcanic sands pounded by the Atlantic give way to the white sandy beaches that stretch northwards up the Caribbean coast. One of them, **Grand Anse Beach**, has won renown for its smooth waters and the silvery whiteness of its 3 km (2 mile) expanse. Some of Grenada's best hotels and restaurants are situated along it, but the beach itself never seems crowded, and it has a desert island air.

Spice Country

Good organized tours from St. George's visit the spice plantations in the northern part of the island. Many people hire a car and undertake the journey on their own, though the poor roads make driving difficult. The route follows the west coast, with bays and headlands of uncommon beauty.

Along the way, you pass Grand Mal Bay, Halifax Harbour, and some of the prettiest fishing villages of Grenada. Hidden among the red roofs of Gouyabe (formerly Charlotte Town) is a **factory** where spices are sorted and dried in preparation for shipping all over the world. Chief among factory products are nutmeg and the mace made from its filament. The heady scents will no doubt tempt you to buy small jars or baskets of fresh spices to take home. To see spices growing on a traditional plantation, head inland a short distance to **Dougaldston Estate**, a centre for the cultivation of nutmeg and cacao.

Other highlights of the north include Sauteurs and nearby Morne du Sauteurs (Leapers' Hill), the rocks from which the last of the hostile Caribs plummeted to death in 1650 rather than surrender to the French. The cliff is not as spectacular as one would imagine, but the rocks about 12 metres (40 feet) below look sufficiently sinister.

Just east lies Levera Bay and its inviting beach, a good place to swim on calm days. Columbus reputedly saw this very place as he passed the little offshore islands of Levera Green and Sandy.

Continue down the eastern coast to **Greville**. Grenada's second-largest town seems more like a casual village than a city, with a lively market and its own spice factory. Turn inland here to return to St. George's, taking the spectacular road with hairpin turns that crosses the island. The many spice plantations in the area can be identified by the red cacao nuts drying in the sun, and you may see boys with cutlasses harvesting the bountiful crops of coconuts, plantains, and nutmeg.

The road passes **Grand Etang National Park**, where the main attraction is an extinct volcano 549 metres (1,800 feet) high that cradles a beautiful blue lake of 5.26 hectares (13 acres). There are trails through the rain forest for hiking, and camping is permitted.

The Forest Centre provides information on the island's wildlife and vegetation. You may want to go (perhaps with a picnic and bathing suit) to **Annandale Falls**, within the perimeters of the park. The 15-metre (50-foot) cascade flows into a stream.

It's like two miles of paradise on the silvery beach in Grand Anse.

Grenada's Grenadines

Both Carriacou (37 km/23 miles northeast of Grenada) and Petit Martinique (3 km/3 miles east of Carriacou) come under the jurisdiction of Grenada. Regular boat services operate here, and there are air connections from several islands to Carriacou. Ample, if fairly simple, hotel accommodation is available only on Carriacou.

Carriacou (pronounced CARRY-COO) has won the acclaim of yachtsmen for its hospitality, which becomes positively raucous during boat launchings or the August Regatta. The French originally settled the island, planting sugar cane and building roads all over Carriacou's 34 square km (13 square miles). But the British coveted the place and finally wrested it from the French in the 18th century.

Today, the legacy of France lives on in the persistence of French place names and the patois spoken by the islanders. Most of the inhabitants are descendants of African slaves or

The spice of life — a local factory worker oversees the production of nutmeg and other spices in Gouyave.

emigrants from Scotland. Those whose names begin in "Mc" are usually employed in boat building.

The sleepy "big" town, **Hillsborough**, wakes up at Regatta time. The rest of the year the island is left to sailors and snorkellers. People travel here just for a look at the area's spectacular coral reefs.

Petit Martinique can count no more than 600 inhabitants, mostly of French descent, though English is spoken. Islanders are known both for their maritime prowess and their boat building. Smuggling is said to be an important occupation, too. Sailors may take refuge in the harbour, but there is no tourist accommodation here

Other fairly deserted and beautiful islands popular with the yachting set include Ile de Ronde, Kick 'em Jenny (supposedly a corruption of *Quai qui gêne* or "Annoying Reef"), Conference, and Green Bird.

TRINIDAD AND TOBAGO

Opposites do attract, especially, when they're neighbours, as Trinidad and Tobago, the southernmost of the Southern Caribbean islands. They're only 32 km (20 miles) apart; they have one government and speak as one nation. The combined population is 1,350,000, some 50,000 of whom represent Tobago. Their union is something of a marriage of convenience, for the two islands were joined artificially in 1889, after Tobago's sugar industry collapsed and the island needed Trinidad's support.

These islands are as different as oil and water. Life in business-oriented Trinidad revolves around Port-of-Spain, the sophisticated capital. Blessed with large oil reserves, the larger island tensely follows the ups and downs of OPEC prices. Tobago proves a more restful and seductive place, with an abundance of natural beauty and pleasant resorts to attract holidaymakers. The two islands complement each other, and it is interesting to see them in turn.

Trinidad

Take an island with rich natural resources and lush scenery, people it with a vast selection of races and faiths, add plenty of steel-band music—and you have a thumbnail sketch of Trinidad.

The island covers a large area of 4,828 square km (1,864 square miles) about 80 by 56 km (50 by 35 miles). It probably broke away from Venezuela in a distant geological age, a theory given credence by the striking similarities in rock formations, flora, and fauna between Trinidad and Venezuela, which lies some 11 km (7 miles) to the south.

Historical Highlights

Columbus himself named Trinidad in 1498—for both the Holy Trinity and the triple mountain peaks he could see from his ship. Spain founded a rather half-hearted colony on the island in 1532, but Trinidad remained poor and largely undeveloped. Sir Walter Raleigh chanced by in 1595 and burned down most of the newly founded Spanish town of San Jose. He also happened upon Pitch Lake—a marsh that provided excellent caulking for his ships. Pitch Lake still supplies asphalt for roads the world over.

During the next hundred years, the number of Spanish colonizers dwindled to about 30. Then new settlers arrived, bringing with them black African slaves to work extensive coffee, sugar cane, cacao, and cotton plantations. New blood and energy flowed into the island in response to a 1783 Spanish royal proclamation calling upon Roman Catholics of all nationalities to settle and work on Trinidad. This encouraged the ethnic diversity that still characterizes the island.

Spanish Trinidad was captured by the British in 1797, although Spain did not concede the change in ownership until 1802. The island became a British colony, loyal to the Crown.

When slavery was abolished in 1833, the former slaves went inland to set up small farms. Thousands of indentured labourers were recruited to replace them, resulting in an influx of Hindus, Muslims, and Parsis from India and the Far East. Today these labourers' descendents make up over one-third of the island's population.

The collapse of the sugar market in 1884 bankrupted neighbouring Tobago, and the island was subsequently

The Red House in Port-of-Spain, built in 1906, is now the seat of the government.

joined to Trinidad in 1889. Early this century, oil was discovered on Trinidad.

While World War I did not affect the islands greatly, the United States built bases on Trinidad during World War II to safeguard the Caribbean.

As a Crown Colony, Trinidad had been given a small measure of self-rule, but further independence was requested by both Trinidad and Tobago. On August 31, 1962, Trinidad-Tobago was officially declared independent. The two islands became a republic in 1976, while continuing as a parliamentary democracy. There are 15 members of parliament from Trinidad and three from Tobago. The chief executive is the president.

Tobago has traditionally felt itself overshadowed by the larger and richer island of Trinidad, and there have been calls for their separation. Although Trinidad still has the oil and the money, the election of a Tobagonian prime minister in 1987 largely defused this situation.

Some cheerful city youngsters.

Port-of-Spain

Lush green hills surround the capital of Trinidad-Tobago. The multi-racial inhabitants live in everything from shacks to imposing colonial palaces. The architecture embraces a variety of styles from neo-Gothic to glossy contemporary, and the restaurants vary from French or Indian to fast food. Port-of-Spain is dotted with parks of all shapes and sizes which Trinidadians like to compare to London's. However, the similarity between England and Trinidad ends with cricket, and you'll never doubt for a moment that you're in the tropics.

Traffic fills streets already busy with vendors and their carts piled high with coconuts and cashew nuts. And though the pace of city life can be hectic, Trinidadians can always find time to take a break, and have made hanging out with friends into an art form known locally as liming.

Begin your exploration of the city on **Frederick Street**, a main artery lined with **shops** that runs from north to south between Queen's Park Savannah (see pages 66-68) and the port. As you walk from the Savannah, you pass the modern Town Hall at the corner of Knox Street.

Next you come to **Woodford Square**, a large green space. Take a right at Knox Street and continue along the square to **Red House**, a stately colonial building (1906) that is now the seat of government. The elaborate bi-coloured stone building nearby on Edward Street is neither a fortress nor a mosque, but rather the central police headquarters. Now cross back to Frederick Street along the south side of Woodford Square, fronted by the neo-Gothic **Anglican cathedral**. Peep inside at its beautifully carved mahogany altar and choir stalls.

The cathedral was built during the early 19th-century governorship of Sir Ralph Woodford, after whom the square was named. Noted worshippers at the cathedral have included the

English writer Charles Kingsley, who describes the Christmas he spent in Trinidad in his book *At Last!*

The section of Frederick Street near the harbour is closed to traffic, and hawkers selling souvenirs congregate in the area, urging passersby to part with their money. The bustling crowds and the colourful scene extend to Independence Square, a wide double thoroughfare thronged with tourists seeking bargains in the big duty-free shops. The street, fortuitously laid out by the Spanish as a military parade ground, serves admirably as an assembly point for participants in Carnival parades, the biggest event of the Trinidad year.

The banks on almost every corner symbolize Trinidad's financial importance. A statue in memory of Andrew Cipriani, a World War I hero and former mayor, stands in Brian Lara Promenade, the tree-lined avenue dividing the parallel streets; another a short distance away is dedicated to Columbus.

The **Roman Catholic cathedral** is situated here, too. This simple stone structure with two bell towers and a woodvaulted interior dates from 1844. Local people keep in voice year-round for Carnival, and services and choir rehearsals are often enlivened by a definite calypso beat.

From Independence Square you might go down to the waterfront, where tourist ships dock, and the Central Market in the Beetham Highway, a lively display of West Indian produce (early in the morning).

Queen's Park Savannah

This magnificent park, complete with race course, playing fields, and plenty of food stands, occupies some 81 hectares (200 acres). Start your visit on the south side at the **National Museum and Art Gallery** on the corner of Frederick and Keate streets. Two Spanish cannon commemorating the

British capture of Trinidad in 1797 and a big anchor supposedly lost by Columbus' fleet lure visitors inside.

To the right of the entrance stands a puncheon, one of the big barrels used in the manufacture of Angostura Bitters, a concoction invented as a cure for stomach upset in 1824 in Venezuela. Later the manufacturing plant was moved to Trinidad. Many of the exhibits are disappointing (minerals and woebegone stuffed specimens of local mammals), but persevere to see the exhibition of gaudy Carnival floats and costumes—insects, snakes, dragons, and devils with enough net, sequins, and feathers to make a cabaret artist jealous. Interesting, too, is a display of snake-bite cures. Paintings by local artists are sometimes on view, many excellent, some of them offered for sale at reasonable prices.

Head north along Maraval Road, the site of Queen's Royal College, a British legacy. The exterior of this boys' school is painted a colourful red and yellow. Continue past an extraordinary collection of old **mansions**, including the residences of the Anglican bishop (blue and cream) and Catholic archbishop (Spanish style). In between stands Roodal's House, decorated in a frothy Creole style that belies its local description of "French Second Empire."

Farther along you come to Whitehall, a Moorish-style structure that serves as the Prime Minister's office. Don't miss Stollmeyer Castle, a white elephant of a house that belonged to a German family. This turreted stone affair has been bought and restored by the government and is now an art gallery.

The quiet little zoo on the northern side of the Savannah contains chimpanzees and colourful birds with bright feathers, as well as misleadingly benign-looking Cayman alligators and restless ocelots.

The **Botanic Gardens** next door prove more interesting, especially if you hire a guide. The 28-hectare (70-acre) gardens were founded in 1818 by one of Trinidad's governors, Sir Ralph Woodford. The trees are clearly labelled, but in any case the ever-helpful guides will be glad to explain everything—from frangipani and sausage trees to the raw beef tree, which seems to bleed when you cut into the bark. There's also a peepul (bo) tree, the type under which Buddha achieved enlightenment. Adjoining the gardens is the stately President's Palace, formerly the Governor-General's residence, a Caribbean version of the neo-Renaissance.

Outskirts of Town

The view of town from **Fort George** merits the bumpy ride uphill over a narrow, potholed road. The small house at the top of the fort overlooks the whole of Paria Bay, taking in the Trinidad Regimental Headquarters, Carrera Island (a prison), and a former leper colony off to the right. On a clear day you can see all the way to Venezuela from this 335-metre (1,100-foot) vantage point.

More sweeping views can be had from the chapel dedicated to Our Lady of Laventille, 5 km (3 miles) from town in the **Laventille Hills**. Spanish-built Fort Chacon (1784) is visible to the north and Fort Picton (1800), English-built, to the south.

You can reach the **Caroni Swamp and Bird Sanctuary**, about 11 km (7 miles) south of Port-of-Spain, by road or boat. Tour companies organize relaxing afternoon excursions by boat, very pleasant except for the hard seats (cushions are not provided). You travel along the Wayama River past endless mangrove trees, their tangle of long roots alive with tiny crabs and oysters.

The Queen's Royal College carries on Britain's tradition of all-boys schools.

QUEEN'S ROYAL
COLLEGE
1904

Mangroves shade a quiet beach.

Magnificent blue and white heron and other birds nest in the sanctuary, but the climax of the tour comes at sunset. Hundreds of scarlet ibis, like wispy clouds of flame, fill the sky with their bright-red feathers. When the birds settle at last on the mangroves, they transform them into Christmas trees heavy with ornament.

Island Sights

You can drive yourself around the island, but it is more enjoyable to hire a car and driver for sightseeing, whether for a morning, an afternoon, or a full day. Certain group excursions prove less expensive than car hire; ask at your hotel or the Tourist Board.

Well worth a visit is **Lopinot**, a cacao estate in the mountains near Arima. Established by a French nobleman fleeing the Revolution, it gives a fascinating glimpse into the life of an 18th-century planter. A river tumbles through the groves and the views are idyllic.

A trip to **Maracas Beach**, one of the most popular swimming areas on the island and the best near the capital, makes another pleasant outing. Drive uphill past the Trinidad Country Club and Moka Golf Course to the North Coast Road, or Skyline Drive. There are panoramic views from the hilly area called The Saddle. Ask your driver to point out highlights of Trinidad vegetation: cacao plants, variegated hibiscus, and teak, nutmeg, and wild silk cotton trees. During the Christmas season you'll see big candle-shaped blossoms on the towering piper tree, called a life plant because it oozes red sap when cut.

You soon cross the foothills of the Northern Range, which afford a view of the sea as far as Tobago. From here, the road runs downhill to Maracas Beach, where swimming is easy, though life guards are on duty in case of trouble. There are changing rooms, and snacks and drinks are available. Then you can drive on to **Las Cuevas**, the next bay along. If you dislike crowds, avoid the beach at weekends.

You could also visit the little town of **Chaguanas** (about a 45-minute drive southeast of Port-of-Spain) in the morning when the food market is in full swing. Here you can see and sample some of the West Indies' most exotic culinary specialities. Try the spicy Indian pastries—fiery but not harmful if your digestion is strong. Every sort of island staple is on sale, from the ugly gilbaca fish and fresh shrimps to dasheen, cassava root, and goats' heads.

One of Trinidad's prime attractions, the **Asa Wright Nature Centre**, lies about an hour's drive east of Port-of-Spain, beyond Piarco Airport. The estate was originally built by German settlers, but the property changed hands and names many times before it was acquired by a state-owned scientific foundation. Tourists are welcome to join the bird watchers, entomologists, and botanists with special scholarly interests, who assemble here to study the flora and fauna of Trinidad. Many people come just to see the oilbird, or guacharo, a rare species that inhabits caves in the grounds.

More guacharos (and diablotins, too) can be seen at the nearby **Aripo Caves**. An array of stalactites and stalagmites adds to the splendour of this little-frequented spot for the adventurous, a few miles northeast of Arima on the Aripo Road. In the distance rise two spectacular mountains, El Cerro del Aripo, 940 metres (3,085 feet), and Chaguaramas, 859 metres (2,817 feet). A visit to the caves can only be recommended to the hardy, since you must walk 4 km (2 1/2 miles) to reach them.

You have to be interested in asphalt to make the three-hour journey by car to **Pitch Lake**, spoken of as one of the wonders of the world. Trinidadians claim that its 91-metre (300-foot) depths provide much of the world's road surfacing. A museum at La Brea relates the history of asphalt and some of the legends associated with Pitch Lake.

The vast, grey "lake" has changed little since its discovery by Sir Walter Raleigh at the end of the 16th century. The surface is generally hard, but it oozes in places and could suck you in like quicksand, so take care in walking around.

Set aside a full day to explore the east coast of Trinidad, a beautiful but little visited region planted with extensive coconut groves. From Port-of-Spain you pass through the scenic interior towns of Valencia and Sangre Grande, reaching the coast at Cocos Bay. Swimming is pleasant on the Bay's two beaches, **Rough** and **Calm Balandra**. You may even bump into a strange species of fish, the "four-eyed" an-

Hauling in the catch is the big event of the day in Trinidad.

ableps. Another sandy beach shaded with a multitude of coconut palms lies farther south at Mayaro Bay.

Tobago

Trinidad's neighbour has been christened "Robinson Crusoe's Island" for no good reason, except that it looks like a place where Defoe's hero might have been stranded. Nearly all of Tobago's 43 by 11 kilometres (26 by 7 miles) provide perfect scenery and relaxation. The island is unspoiled, but like every paradise in a natural state, there are a few drawbacks. You may encounter the occasional water shortage, and a casual attitude and easygoing way of life rarely produce quick service. But you'll forget all about any inconvenience as you sip an exquisitely scented rum punch or swim in the turquoise sea.

Historical Highlights

Tobago takes its name from the tobacco plant, or from the Spanish word for the natives' pipes. Spain was so busy colonizing Trinidad that Tobago was left to itself for at least a hundred years. Then, early in the 17th century, the English attempted to settle the island, but disease and Carib raids decimated the inhabitants.

For the next hundred years or so, Tobago's history was stormy, and the island changed hands between Dutch, French, and English dozens of times. The Dutch invaded in 1658, the English privateers took over (1666), followed the next year by the French, and so on. After the island was declared neutral territory in 1748, French-English rivalry grew even more intense.

Between battles, life went on. Slaves were imported and plantations started. By 1770, when the population numbered some 3,000 Africans and only 200 whites, the first slave uprising had taken place. From 1781 the French held sway, but the British regained control in 1793. The Treaty of Amiens returned Tobago to France in 1802, but not for long. The British were back again in 1803, landing at Arnos Vale Bay. They were aided by a slave called George Winchester, who later won his freedom and became Tobago's first black businessman.

With it all, Tobago became a great sugar-producing colony, giving rise to the local expression "rich as a Tobago planter." When emancipation took place in 1834, slave labour became paid labour after a fashion. In spite of a disastrous hurricane in 1847, sugar, rum, and cotton production boomed. Rich little Tobago was made a Crown Colony in

1877. But prosperity came to an abrupt end in 1884 when the sugar market collapsed. As a result of the economic disaster, Tobago was made a ward of Trinidad five years later.

Along with Trinidad, Tobago gained independence in 1962. Although construction and development has brought change to the island, Tobago has kept a great deal of its primitive aspect and charm. Whether this will survive the arrival of intercontinental flights at the new airport remains to be seen.

Scarborough

Tobago's capital, a sleepy little town of 17,000 on the southwest coast, lies about 16 km (10 miles) from the airport and a good 30 minutes from most resort hotels. Scarborough looks like a shantytown when public works are underway, as is often the case, but it's a friendly place.

Sugar cane makes its way from the fields to production.

A quaint gingerbread house—the full bloom in the front yard rivals other colourful gardens on Tobago.

Fort King George (completed 1779), the principal sight, stands above Scarborough. From its 137-metre (450-foot) elevation you can see Bacolet, a prosperous residential area, and Trinidad. Both the island's hospital and the former prison are situated downhill from the fort. The once-formidable prison was the scene of a revolt in 1801 that ended in the sentencing to death of 39 prisoners. According to legend, the governor was loath to carry out so many executions, but to save face he ordered that one body be strung up over and over again.

The fort bears witness to French-English rivalry for the island, and a plaque commemorates every change of fortune: France 1781, Great Britain 1793, and on the list goes. A bronze cannon from the period of George III remains in place, and there are plenty of exotic plants to admire, especially in the peaceful garden of a ruined church on the site.

Southwest of Scarborough, head southwest in the direction of the airport. You pass excellent sandy beaches, often with hardly anyone in sight. This is an inviting place to snorkel and go swimming in the surf. For a nominal admission you can enjoy the spectacular stretch of fine sand at **Pigeon Point**, near the swampy Bon Accord Lagoon. There are changing rooms, cabanas, and a simple bar-restaurant.

Buccoo Reef, an extensive coral reef that is one of Tobago's main attractions, lies about a mile offshore from Pigeon Point and Bon Accord Lagoon. Glass-bottom boats reveal the wonders of the warm tropical sea, and you'll marvel at the Queen trigger-fish, blue tang, yellowtail, snapper, and other beauties of the deep. For a clear view underwater, be sure to make the trip on a fair day at low tide. Swimmers can use the boat's snorkel equipment, and there are rubber-soled sandals for protection against coral cuts and sea urchins.

You may want to make use of the beach facilities at the **Mount Irvine Bay Hotel**, a luxury installation to the north, or its 18-hole golf course, one of the best in the Caribbean. Non-residents are welcome.

Towards the Caribbean

A scenic road leads northwest of Scarborough, passing **Fort William**, a well-maintained red-brick building that serves as the official residence of the Trinidad-Tobago president. Farther along you'll see a plantation Great House called The Whim. Not long afterwards you arrive at the town of **Plymouth** on the coast. A tombstone in Plymouth was inscribed in 1793 with a puzzling epitaph in memory of Betty Stivens: "She was a mother without knowing it and a wife, without letting her husband know, except by her kind indulgences to him." Islanders translate this as a classic love story between a master and his black mistress. She was the mother of the man's children, and was honoured by marriage to him only after her death, when the master also recognized the children.

The **Great Courland Bay Monument**, situated on a point, commands a striking view of the sea, and there is good swimming from the beach below. The monument was erected in memory of "the enterprising and industrious Courlanders from faraway Batavia on the Baltic shores, who lived in this area..." The cannon nearby mark the site of Fort James, built in 1768.

Continue northeast along the coast to the **Arnos Vale Hotel**, a former sugar plantation. Before this road was improved, some drivers refused to attempt it. A disused sugar mill fitted out with a formidable crushing wheel made in Glasgow in 1857 stands in the grounds. Some of the guest rooms are situated in the gracious plantation house, and an 18th-century clavichord lends its elegance to the sitting room.

☛ The event of the day at Arnos Vale is **bird-watching** at tea-time. This pleasant activity will never tire you, for while you sit and sip your tea, the birds flock to you: the yellow breasted bananaquit, Tobago blue tanager, ruby topaz hummingbird, and handsome, orange-breasted king of the woods or mot-mot. In just one afternoon you can become an amateur ornithologist.

Not far away at Grafton Estate you can also watch the birds. For either place, go around 4:00 P.M., the best time to see and feed the birds.

From Arnos Vale, poor roads lead northeast to Charlotteville, a fishing town, but a good local driver will have no trouble negotiating the turns. Scenic highlights include precipitous views of headlands and the sea, alternating with picturesque huts on stilts serving as bars, stores, or post offices. There are good swimming beaches at Castara Bay, Englishman's Bay and Parlatuvier, a fishing village with pastel houses.

Trinidad-Tobago Briefing

Airports. Trinidad's Piarco International Airport is 30 km (18 miles) east of Port-of-Spain. Taxis are always available (the ride in to the city is about 45 minutes). The flight from Piarco to Crown Point Airport on Tobago takes about 12 minutes.

Currency. Trinidad-Tobago dollar (TT$), 100 cents = TT$1. Issued in 1, 5, 10, 20, and 100-dollar notes and coins of 1, 5, 10, 25, and 50 cents.

Electric Current. 115 or 230 volts, 60 cycle AC.

Emergencies. Dial 999 for police, 990 for ambulance and fire.

Hospitals. Trinidad:Mount Hope Hospital, 164 Charlotte Street, Port-of-Spain, tel. 62-32951. Tobago: Scarborough General, tel. 639-2500

Hours. General business and shopping hours: Monday to Thursday 8 a.m. to 4 or 4:30 p.m., Friday 8 a.m. to 6 p.m., Saturday 8 a.m. to noon. Banking hours: Monday to Thursday 9 a.m. to 2 p.m., Friday 8 a.m. to noon and 3 to 5 p.m.

Newspapers. Three dailies, the *Guardian*, *Newsday*, and the *Express*.

Public Holidays. New Year's Day (January 1), Eid-ul-Fitr (Moslem festival, movable), Carnival (unofficial, Monday and Tuesday preceding Ash Wednesday), Good Friday and Easter Monday (movable), Whit Monday (movable), Corpus Christi (movable), Labour Day (June 19), Independence Day (August 31), Divali (Hindu festival, movable), Christmas and Boxing Day (December 25 and 26).

Trinidad and Tobago Tourist Boards
Trinidad: 10-14 Phillipps Street, Port-of-Spain, tel. 623-6022/3
Tobago: IDC Mall, Sangster's Hill, Scarborough, tel. 639-4333
U.K.: 66 Abbey Road, Bush Hill, Enfield, Middlesex EN1 2RQ, tel: (020) 8350 1000
Canada: Taurus House, 512 Duplex Avenue, Toronto M4R 2E3, Ontario, tel. (416) 485 8724
U.S.A.:350 Fifth Avenue, New York, NY 10118, tel. 212-760 2400

You may want to make a detour inland to the **Tobago Forest Reserve**, where trails invite long hikes. Ask for good maps and information at the Tourist Board in Scarborough. In the Charlottesville region are the sandy beach at Man O'War Bay and Pigeon Peak, the island's highest point at nearly 3,600 metres (2,000 feet). A road links the town to Speyside on the Atlantic.

Atlantic Sights

Take the scenic road that travels east from Scarborough along the wild Atlantic coast. The drive to Speyside takes two or three hours. Tiny villages like Mesopotomia, Goldsborough, and Roxborough line the way. You may want to stop for a swim at one of the bays just before Roxborough: Prince's, Queen's, or King's.

Continue to Speyside, a colourful beach settlement. From here you can see tiny Goat Island and **Little Tobago**, a 182-hectare (450-acre) bird sanctuary, also known as Bird-of-Paradise Island. To see the birds at close range, take a boat to the island from Speyside, a one-hour trip. In addition to the native birds that congregate here, there are dozens of other species, including gilt-plumed birds-of-paradise.

A cocorico, the national bird of Trinidad-Tobago, blends into its surroundings.

WHAT TO DO

SPORTS

The Southern Caribbean islands, famed haunts of beachcombers and yachtsmen, offer an array of sports possibilities as dazzling as the sand, sea, and sunshine. You can jog along the firm, sandy beaches, swim, sunbathe, and sail, or search the coral reefs for beautiful underwater views. If you observe the usual sun and heat precautions you'll return home relaxed and healthy.

There's an island for every sport. Resorts on Barbados, Grenada, St. Vincent, and, to a lesser extent, Tobago hire out equipment and provide instructors. Parasailing and water-skiing are tops on Barbados and St. Lucia. In the Grenadines, however, there are fewer sports facilities, but many glorious beaches. While Trinidad has a great deal to

Water sports are the best on beaches such as Young Island, just 200 yards off the St. Vincent shore.

offer the tourist, the best hotels are situated inland, and the atmosphere is not really holiday orientated in the sense of beaches and watersports. Day cruises to areas good for snorkeling operate on most islands.

Watersports

Beaches and Swimming

Miles of sandy beaches, usually golden or silvery-white, rim the islands. There are some volcanic black-sand beaches on St. Vincent and Grenada, but these prove more popular with sightseers than with swimmers. The islands' beaches are open to everyone, but you may be expected to pay for a mat or a chair at beaches developed by resort hotels.

Some swimming areas are roped off for good reason: there may be a dangerous undertow, sharp-cutting coral, or sea urchins there. Make sure of swimming conditions and the

Underwater Wonderland

A host of exotic creatures inhabits the watery depths of the Caribbean. Common sights include elkhorn, finger, and brain coral, which look exactly as their names imply. In addition, you may see fire and pillar coral, as well as sea fans. Take care not to step on the razor-sharp coral, and refrain from breaking off samples, a practice frowned upon by the authorities.

Fish are not at all shy about parading their gorgeous colours past snorkellers and divers. Look for the bright-blue-and-yellow queen angelfish, the orange-and-blue honeytail damselfish, and striking queen triggerfish. The blue ocean surgeon has a neat "incision" marked in black on its gill, and the sergeant-major sports pretty blue, yellow, and black stripes.

Come on in, the water's great! Scuba diving is easy, fun, and safe — after a few simple lessons.

availability of a life-guard before taking small children or learners into the water. The windy Atlantic beaches are washed by a wild and woolly surf dangerous for all but very good swimmers. There are big waves, and experts can surf in some places.

Outstanding beaches are to be found along the St. James coast (Barbados); at Choc Bay, Vigie Beach, and Marigot Beach (St. Lucia); Grand Anse Beach and Levera (Grenada); and Pigeon Point (Tobago). There are adequate beaches at the resort hotels near Kingstown (St. Vincent), but these are far surpassed by the idyllic strands of the Grenadines, too numerous to list.

Snorkeling

A passion with many island visitors, snorkeling is particularly good off Tobago (especially Buccoo Reef), Barbados, St. Vincent, Grenada, and most of the Grenadines.

There are guided snorkel tours on many islands. Equipment is sold almost everywhere. Diving services and some hotels hire out masks and flippers, other hotels loan masks and flippers free of charge.

Scuba Diving

Lightweight diving equipment will enable you to see a whole new underwater world—from shipwrecks to strange and beautiful fish. There are diving centres on many islands, and hotels often provide scuba (an acronym for Self-Contained Underwater Breathing Apparatus) facilities. A three-day introductory course, including classroom study, is usually compulsory for beginners.

Other Watersports

Many resort beaches hire out motorboats and drivers for water-skiing. Instruction is often available. Some of St. Lucia's major hotels include 15 minutes of water-skiing (and a half-hour of sailing) daily in the price of the room. Otherwise, you'll have to pay by the hour or day; prices vary considerably from island to island.

Windsurfing is becoming increasingly popular, and equipment for this strenuous, demanding exercise in balance now exists at many resorts. Barbados specializes in parasailing, a thrilling extension of water-skiing. Towed by a motorboat, you take off from a floating launch wearing a harness fitted with a parachute. You soar into the air for a few minutes and land again on the launch. It's harmless fun for anyone in good health who likes heights.

Deep-Sea Fishing

The best season for game fish runs from November to April. Depending on where you are, you can catch blue or white marlin, barracuda, kingfish, dolphin, and wahoo. Up to six fishermen can charter a small boat, and local fishermen, especially around St. Vincent and the Grenadines, often permit enthusiasts to join them in a hard day's work. You have to set out at about 3:00 A.M., but you'll certainly catch plenty of edible varieties this way.

Boats and Sailing

Hiring small sailboats (called sunfish), motorboats, catamarans, or other vessels is a simple matter in the Southern Caribbean, and there is often no other way to reach deserted islands, coves, and nearby reefs. You can arrange to charter a yacht on St. Lucia, St. Vincent, or Grenada, the islands with the best facilities and harbours. Depending on the terms of hire, the price may include food, drink, and crew's wages. Many yacht charters allow you to "cruise and learn" with sailing instruction from the crew. Ask at the various tourist offices for information.

Sports Ashore

Tennis

There is no shortage of courts on the islands. Many hotels have built their own, others offer unlimited access to courts nearby. Non-residents can often play on private hotel courts on payment of a hire charge. There are several public courts on Trinidad and Barbados, most of them are just as good as the hotel courts, for half the price.

Golf

Clubs on the major islands readily admit visitors for a small fee. You can generally hire equipment and the services of a caddy. Try the fine 18-hole course at Sandy Lane

A British legacy, cricket remains a favourite game on the islands. Here is a match in Port-of-Spain.

(Barbados) or the Barbados Golf and Country Club at Christ Church.

In good British tradition, Trinidad and Tobago have eight golf courses between them, including Moka, Brighton, and Point-a-Pierre. Tobago's 18-hole Mount Irvine course is the site of professional tournaments

On St. Lucia, there are pleasant and scenic nine-hole courses at Cap Estate Golf Club and Hotel La Toc. St. Vincent's nine-hole Aquaduct course is situated in an attractive tropical setting about half an hour by car from Kingstown. The Woodlands, on Grenada, offers views of the Atlantic and the Caribbean with every putt.

Horseback Riding

Canter along scenic trails on Barbados and St. Lucia, the only islands in the Southern Caribbean where riding facilities are available. Stables in the Barbados parishes of St.

Michael's and St. Thomas are readily accessible to resort-hotel guests. There are many scenic trails, especially around Sam Lord's Castle. St. Lucia's riding is from Cap Estate in the northwest to Pigeon Island and other places of great natural beauty.

Spectator Sports

Enthusiasm for cricket has never waned in this former British enclave, especially on Barbados, where the season runs from June to January. Matches are played at the Kingston Oval.

Football (soccer) has its devotees, and on Barbados and Trinidad polo attracts large crowds. In addition, there are horse races held two to four times yearly on Barbados, Trinidad, and Tobago.

Hiking

There are countless places to explore in the jungles and hills of Trinidad, Tobago, St. Lucia, Grenada, and St. Vincent. In fact, you can only reach St. Vincent's Soufrière volcano by foot (see page 37). It's a good idea to hire a competent guide, except perhaps on Barbados, where the gentle terrain makes for ease of walking. Be sure to bring sturdy shoes.

SHOPPING

Several islands offer outstanding duty-free bargains in luxury goods such as jewellery and china, but shops in Barbados probably offer the widest range of items and the best service. Look for establishments labelled "in-bond" or "duty-free." Tax-free purchases are sealed and delivered to you after you've gone through customs at the airport or dock. You can also send tax-free goods by mail, but the postage may be prohibitively expensive.

Every island also produces a good deal of craft work, though specialities vary from place to place. Hand-crafted articles are available in regular shops or on the beach, where prices are cheaper and a little bargaining is part of the fun.

Works of art by local artists include colourful primitive painting and attractive African-style woodcarving and sculpture. Ask tourist offices or hotel staff for the addresses of the best galleries and workshops.

Wherever you go, you'll find a selection of small souvenirs, from elaborate, costumed dolls in ruffled dresses to straw articles. Postage stamps make another worthy memento of the islands, since each nation produces its own beautiful designs.

Here is what to look out for on the various islands:

Barbados

Shops generally open on weekdays from 8:00 A.M. to 4:00 P.M., Saturdays 8:00 A.M. to noon. There are smart boutiques all over the island, especially in or near the resort hotels. The main shopping street in Bridgetown is Broad Street.

Duty-free buys include transistor radios, cameras, and Swiss watches, as well as a selection of china, glass, and crystal. You'll also find tobacco, cigarettes, perfume, and spirits, with Barbados rum a bestseller. For last-minute shoppers, the Barbados airport has some nice, small duty-free shops.

Clothing for men and women is available in cashmeres, cottons, silks, and accessories. A few tailors will stitch up suits for men in a few days. Women's sports clothes are good, whether sold in boutiques or on the beaches.

You can buy excellent beach-wear where you bathe from colourful little racks set up daily (except Sundays) by local seamstresses. Men and women both like the brightly printed unisex overblouses, and women may want to purchase at least one airy sarong, which can be tied in various ways.

One of the islands' handcrafted treasures: copper work from Trinidad.

There are also comfortable long caftans and pretty sundresses. Most styles come in sizes for children.

Handicraft items typical of Barbados include reed or straw place mats, sisal or straw bags and baskets, and various articles (jewellery in particular) made from seashells and coral; ceramics are also available. In some shops, good batik is sold —for a price. Beware of washing the cloth, which isn't always colour-fast.

St. Lucia

Main shops open weekdays, except Wednesday, 8:00 A.M. to noon and 1:00 to 4:00 P.M., Wednesday 8:00 A.M. to 12 noon, Saturday, 9:00 A.M. to 1:00 P.M. A couple of shops in Castries sell very nice print and batik sportswear for women, and there are boutiques selling clothes and souvenirs in the better hotels. You can carry home the heady scent of tropical flowers in the form of locally blended perfume.

Dolls, pretty stamps, and shell necklaces are sold everywhere, and you'll also see beaded jewellery, small carved wooden objects, and the usual local straw and sisal articles: bags, baskets, hats, and rugs.

St. Vincent

Shops are open Monday to Friday, 8:00 A.M. to noon, and 1:00 to 4:00 P.M., and on Saturdays from 8:00 A.M. to noon only. Apart from the usual duty-free spirits and perfume, there is also a small selection of crystal and china. Local crafts items are similar to those of St. Lucia: straw and

Local artisans shape and craft wood carvings in St. Lucia.

sisal goods, carved wooden objects, and coral necklaces. Some of the batik sold here is of very high quality.

On all of the populated Grenadines, you'll find small souvenirs and sportswear. Particularly useful on these islands are the green palm frond sun hats, woven for you on the beach.

Grenada

Shopping hours are 8:00 to 11:45 a.m. and 1:00 to 4:00 p.m. Monday to Friday and 8:00 a.m. to noon Saturdays. The most obvious buys on the Spice Island are spice baskets woven of straw or palm fronds and filled with ginger, cinnamon, nutmeg and so on. Near the market in the centre of St. George's, you'll find all sorts of hand-crafted goods, from hand-blown glass to straw hats, bags, and mats. There are also many shops selling china, spirits, and other duty-free goods. Certain shops and hotel boutiques sell very attractive batik caftans and overblouses, as well as resort wear in African or Liberty cottons.

Look, too, for tortoise-shell objects and jewellery, china, and ceramics. A few shops stock excellent British woollens and cashmeres—if you can face choosing winter clothing m the tropics. There are also a couple of galleries selling the best of island art.

Trinidad and Tobago

Shopping hours are 8:00 a.m. to 4:00 p.m. Monday to Thursday; 8:00 a.m. to 6:00 p.m. Friday and 8:00 a.m. to noon Saturday. Port-of-Spain's best shops are in Frederick Street, Independence Square, and in or near luxury hotels.

Duty-free goods include a wide selection of cameras, binoculars, watches, perfumes, and spirits. There are also some cashmere, Shetland, and silk items, though not in great abundance. Larger shops stock china, crystal, glass, and silver.

A few shops specializing in men's custom tailoring can make a suit in a few days' time. In general, resort and town clothing for women isn't up to the standard of the other islands, though Indian silks, cotton shirts, and caftans could be good buys, and typical loose shirts can be picked up in the street for a song.

Other popular buys include a vast array of silver and gold filigree Indian-style jewellery. Many visitors pick up a chiselled gold or silver bangle bracelet or two, like those worn by Trinidadian women.

There are many local handicrafts for sale, such as carved Indian or African-style wooden or ivory statues and figurines. Woven straw and fibre objects range from little boxes to attractive fish-shaped place mats, shoulder bags, and carryalls. The sisal and straw furniture is good-looking, but you must be able to transport it home. The selection of costumed dolls reflects Trinidad in all its variegated glory— with rich sari-clad Hindu dolls, ruffled dancing girls, and fanciful Carnival performers.

If you like island music, buy your own "pan," or steel drum, and learn to play it. And, of course, to evoke the total sound, you can buy excellent recordings of calypso, steelband, and Carnival tunes.

For the best Trinidadian painting and sculpture, go to the Port-of-Spain Museum, where works of art are sometimes sold, or ask your hotel or the tourist board for the names of reputable galleries.

Tobago is not really a place to shop, though you can find a few interesting local souvenirs like shells, tortoise objects, and dolls, as well as a small selection of luxury goods and sportswear in the larger hotels.

ENTERTAINMENT

Carnival

All the Southern Caribbean islands celebrate their version of Carnival at various times of year. Trinidad's traditional Carnival is an eye-opening display on a vast scale. It was originally a French custom, brought to the islands by French immigrants in the 18th century. At first the festival was a rather dignified expression of jollity, with masked balls, *fêtes champêtres*, and

A beautiful dancer shows her true colours at a Carnival Queen Show in St. Vincent.

Steelband...

This unmistakable sound is known all over the world—beautiful music from oil drums. It all started in Trinidad in 1937, when a ragtag group led by "Lord Humbugger" marched into Port-of-Spain during a carnival parade playing "pans" to an enraptured crowd. Soon budding musicians all over the island were shaping and tuning steel oil drums. At first there was disapproval of the jumbled jazz being produced in the shanty towns. World War II interrupted activity, but post-war bands came out in force. Players hailed from all walks of life, though most of them were seeking a creative outlet from the poverty of the slums.

Steelband music was refined more and more, and today a "pan tuner" commands a good deal of respect. He tempers the metal with heat, then hammers it with a sledge hammer, taking care to make indentations that will produce the best steelband sounds when struck with mallets.

Steelband is now a musical way of life all over the Caribbean, and the compositions and range of tones can be astonishing. From the latest popular hits to unique renditions of Mozart or Bach, every band takes pride in its own special repertoire.

...and Calypso

Trinidadians also take credit for inventing this special form of music, with its catchy rhythm and witty (sometimes suggestive) lyrics. Calypso evolved over a period of more than 200 years, though songs weren't written in English until the turn of the century.

The word "calypso" probably derives from "cariso," a song-and-dance act performed by women between men's duelling acts during Carnival, though the word may have its origin in "kaiso," a West African dance-chorus. The music combines slave songs and African rhythms with French, Spanish, and Irish musical traditions, not to mention some Chinese and Indian elements.

Harry Belafonte popularized calypso in songs like "Matilda" and "Little Bird." There are many types of calypso, including songs for work and play, shango or popular religious songs and songs of revolt. What you hear today is often a sophisticated mix of political and personal observation, not always easy to understand if you don't know the local dialects and expressions.

carriage promenades. But things began to swing after Emancipation in 1834, when freed slaves took part.

They brought with them *canboulay* (from cannes brûlées—a celebration associated with the old plantation custom of burning off cane stalks left in the fields after harvest). New rhythms and music of Spanish and African origin were introduced, as well as unconventional musical instruments made of bamboo, gourds, and bottles.

Local musicians drum out their talent in a steel band.

Fun was fun, but the situation got out of hand on Trinidad when hoodlums joined the ranks and *canboulay* turned into torch-lit riots with stickfighting in 1881. In the 1890s, however, Carnival made a comeback, and competitions for masquerading groups of bands wearing thematic costumes were organized.

Today, tension and excitement build up in the weeks preceding Carnival. Big bands with hundreds and even thousands of participants start rehearsing in earnest just after the New Year, and the public can buy tickets to rehearsals. Carnival itself is limited to a mere 43 hours, from 5:00 A.M. Monday (*jour ouvert,* or "opening day") to midnight Shrove Tuesday. Everyone celebrates in wild abandon, literally collapsing as Ash Wednesday dawns.

Port-of-Spain's Carnival opens with "Ole Mas," the crowning of the King of Carnival, and the first big bands shuffle into Independence Square during "Lil Mas" Monday afternoon, already dancing to the music. By Monday evening the festivities are in full swing. More costumed bands parade, and spectators pack the streets to join in, carried away body and soul by the compelling rhythms. Plenty of rum is imbibed, and the atmosphere grows euphoric.

Prizes are awarded for music and costumes, but the awed visitor is hardly aware of the finer points. The final day of parades (Mardi Gras) takes place at the Savannah. It's a mind-boggling spectacle of light, sound, and colour, with costumes that make Hollywood extravaganzas look tame.

You might want to avoid the hysteria of the actual celebration and participate in the warm-up during the week or two before Carnival instead. In any case, reserve your hotel and

Nightlife is never dull — there are always traditional costumes and creative spirits to liven up the evening.

parade seats at least a year ahead, if possible. Remember that pickpockets find Carnival ideal for practicing their trade. Leave valuable items in your hotel safe, and take a minimum of money to the parades.

Nightlife

Music swells up in the islands and there's dancing in the dark, in the moonlight, on the streets. Most nightlife revolves around the hotels, which can provide excellent entertainment, from calypso and fire-eaters to slightly more elaborate shows. But the atmosphere is usually rather sedate, with dancing to live music. On some islands there are small cinemas, including a few drive-in theatres. Symphony, opera, and ballet hardly exist, but no one seems to care.

Top pop groups perform on Barbados and Trinidad. Your hotel will know what's on and where. Many islands have a weekly entertainment guide. When you go to a hotel other than your own, you're expected to have at least a drink if there's no entry fee. Sometimes the price of admission includes the first drink.

There are also discos, *boîtes,* low dives, and big outdoor clubs providing floor-shows and musicians to keep you dancing. Barbados offers the biggest choice of nightlife of all the islands in this guide. Groups of calypso dancers, limbo artists, and fire-eaters perform in local night spots. Anyone who is reasonably dressed—usually men don't even need a tie—can gain admission anywhere.

St. Vincent has the Southern Caribbean's only casino, but it's a considerable drive from Kingstown, and often closed. The atmosphere is casual, and there are no special dress requirements. You can play roulette, blackjack, and slot machines, and the low minimum bets must be the most reasonable in the world.

EATING OUT

Picture a fresh catch of fish and shellfish, a multi-coloured choice of glistening and exotic fruits and vegetables, and an aura of spice. This is the essence of Caribbean cooking at its best. Many restaurants make an effort to serve typical Caribbean dishes—the result of a happy marriage of fresh products and time-honoured recipes evolved from the culinary traditions of Africa, Spain, France, India, and England.

Throughout the Southern Caribbean, lunch is served from about noon to 2:00 P.M. and dinner from 7:00 to 10:00 P.M. In addition to hotel restaurants, there is a wide range of eating houses. You can sample highly flavoured East Indian curry dishes or specialities straight from Peking (especially in Trinidad), as well as exotic island fare.

Breakfast

The joy of breakfast is fresh tropical juices and fruits, especially grapefruit, juicy orange pawpaws (papayas), pineapple, mangoes, and watermelon.

For Starters

Before you tackle the menu with its tempting array of specialities, relax with an aperitif or cocktail and crisp plantain chips deep-fried in coconut oil. Plantain—similar in appearance to a green banana but much firmer and not nearly as sweet—makes a good introduction to island tastes.

Among the wide variety of first courses are *pastelles,* plantain or banana leaves stuffed with a corn meal and savoury meat filling. *Accras,* lightly fried herbed codfish balls, can be served with a piquant sauce or (especially in Trinidad) with "floats"—puffy, fried yeast biscuits. In Barbados this dish is called, simply, fishcakes.

Trinidad's *bol-jol,* salt-cod served with pickled cucumber and lime, is available throughout the region.

The more familiar dishes include shrimp salad and fried scampi (particularly delicious on Trinidad and Tobago, but good everywhere), and potato salad.

Soups

The islanders have a gift for concocting delicious soups from local products. Most famous is Trinidad's *callaloo,* more like a full meal than a mere soup. It has become a standard Caribbean dish, though ingredients and spelling may vary

Fresh fruit and vegetables are part of most island meals.

from island to island. The basic recipe calls for *dasheen* leaves (similar to spinach), okra, onions, garlic, chicken stock, salt-pork or beef, coconut milk, crab meat, and hot pepper seasoning to taste.

Here are some soups exotic enough for the most jaded palate: cream of breadfruit (hot or cold), avocado, cream of pumpkin or *christophene* (a local variety of the gourd elsewhere known as squash). Highly spiced pigeon-pea soup is usually made with coconut milk and a little ham or salt-pork.

Black-bean soup is popular, and you can hardly go wrong with cream of crab, an aristocrat among soups on all the islands. There is also fish soup, called bouillabaisse on French islands. Jellied orange or lemon consommé is refreshing on hot days and light enough to please the diet conscious gourmet.

Fish and Seafood

Always ask for the catch of the day in the Caribbean. You'll be tempted by crab backs, crab shells stuffed with a spicy crab-meat filling, a speciality of Trinidad that is available on most islands. Shrimp is wonderful, whether deep-fried in batter, in a cream sauce, or grilled barbecue-style.

Lambi, chewy conch meat, appears on menus in the fishing villages of St. Lucia, St. Vincent, and the Grenadines; it's served cold with lime, having been chopped and pickled beforehand. Conch is also used in curries and soups.

Spiny lobster can misleadingly be referred to as lobster in the Caribbean. It's also called crawfish, *langouste,* and *langosta.* But whatever the name, this tasty crustacean is expensive but good, whether grilled and served with melted butter or cold with herb-flavoured mayonnaise.

Be sure to try flying fish, especially in Barbados: it's lightly fried and served with lime wedges and tartar sauce or cut into fingers and deep fried. The dolphin served in these parts has nothing to do with "Flipper." The small, white-fleshed tropical fish can be prepared in many ways, usually fried or steamed and seasoned with herbs.

Coquilles of fish—shells filled with scallops or billfish—may be served temptingly *au gratin* in a wine-flavoured sauce with mushrooms. Red snapper, scallops, swordfish, and kingfish are prepared in every imaginable way, from sauteed or fried to poached or baked. Sauces can be tangy, and some fish dishes are seasoned with curry spices.

Meat Specialities

Meat is quite popular, though often imported. You'll find good steaks and other cuts of beef—as well as pork and lamb— prepared in all the usual ways with each chef's favourite sauce.

But there is one outstanding meat dish served in various forms all over the islands and especially on Trinidad and Barbados. This speciality, known as pepperpot, reputedly originated with the South American Indians. It's a succulent stew of pork and beef, perhaps even chicken, though the key ingredient in most recipes is *casareep,* a spicy mixture of grated cassava, cinnamon, and brown sugar. Very different is *pelau* (or *pilau*), a Trinidad speciality probably introduced by the Muslims. This rice-based dish combines fish or chicken, pigeon peas, tomatoes, garlic, onions, and plenty of coconut milk, raisins and *garam masala* (curry spices).

If you're lucky enough to see *sancoche,* try it as a main dish. It's a "soup" of pork and pig's tail, with lots of beef and stock, cassava, yams, potatoes, chives, peppers, and perhaps coconut milk. You'll probably agree that it's far too filling to qualify as a starter. Another dish served as appetiz-

Fresh flowers and succulent fruits enrich every meal.

er or entree, pudding and *souse,* combines black pudding (blood sausage) and *souse,* special lime-marinated pig's feet.

Chicken, duck, turkey, and guinea fowl, or *pintadeau,* are served in abundance in the islands. The meat can be stuffed and roasted or served in sauces. *Canard à l'orange* and curried chicken are both delicious. Goat and rabbit are prepared in a variety of interesting and tasty ways by local people in their homes, but you rarely see these meats on menus.

Vegetables

Imaginative cooking does justice to the exotic offerings of Caribbean gardens. Plantains can be cooked as a savoury vegetable. Try warm plantain balls, called *foo-foo* in Guyana and pound plantain in Trinidad. Cucumbers are delicately sauteed, as is *christophene,* a kind of squash. This vegetable can also be cooked au gratin in cream sauce.

Both *dasheen* (the tuberous part) and breadfruit may be boiled, sauteed or fried. Dasheen leaves are used in *callaloo* soup, and breadfruit resembles chestnuts in taste.

Coo-coo technically means a side dish, but this usually implies corn meal or semolina cooked in various ways on the different islands. Barbados and Trinidad-Tobago cooks add okra to the corn meal, combining the ingredients in a mould and serving the dish as an accompaniment to meat as well as fish.

Snacks

There's never a problem if you're hungry between meals, but street-stands may not be the best place to eat if you have a delicate stomach. In Trinidad many stands sell apples (wash them first), plus Indian specialities like deep-fried *kachouris* (chick-pea fritters), *poulouris* (balls of split-pea meal), and *sahinas* (fritters of ground split peas with saffron). Use the accompanying sauces with caution; they can be very potent.

Shops selling chips (French fries) vie with peanut vendors and pizza, corn fritter, and meatball sellers. If you develop a yearning for American-style fast food, you'll be able to find that, too.

Desserts

The wealth of fresh fruit provides a host of refreshing desserts. Mangoes, passion-fruit, grapefruit, bananas, paw-paws, and pineapple are just a few of the possibilities. Fruit salads can be excellent, especially with a dash of liqueur or rum. *Crêpes flambées* may be filled with exotic fruits.

Bananas are served fresh flambéed, fried, and in bread or cakes. *Soursop,* a tangy fruit, is sometimes made into a good ice or a cold drink. Guava cheese, made by boiling the fruit down with sugar till it reaches a jellied consistency when cooled, is found on all the islands.

Gâteaux, or cakes, range from sweet and custard-filled varieties to those made with excellent bitter chocolate. Fruit and liqueurs figure in many recipes. Dessert trolleys often display pies as well, especially a lime pie similar to that made on the Florida Keys, as well as the irresistible frozen lime pie.

Coconut is used liberally in cakes, puddings, cream-filled pies, and tarts. And the English preference for trifle is well catered for, since the rich dessert calls for a liberal dose of rum. St. Vincent restaurants sometimes serve arrowroot custard, a kind of blancmange good with jams and fruits.

Ices and ice creams with a tropical taste include pineapple, coconut, and ginger. If you tire of these, there are many varieties more, like mango, guava, lime—and even soursop for a change from the ordinary.

Drinks

Non-alcoholic island favourites include fruit punch and coconut water from a freshly opened shell. Look for bottled Sorrel, a refreshing bright-red spicy drink that's made from a local plant called rosella. Mauby, another popular concoction, is made from roots and bark, with cinnamon, clove, and other spices. On Barbados you can sip the drink at a street stand, or take concentrate home to mix with water to your own taste.

While spirits and wine are available everywhere, the prices vary widely. Many hotel restaurants serve table wines by the glass, but prices can escalate. The local beer is usually reasonably priced and good, as some islands brew their own—Banks (Barbados), Carib (Trinidad), Heineken (St. Lucia)—but the obvious drink is rum.

Each bartender has his own recipe for rum punch, which is often sprinkled liberally with nutmeg—an idea from Grenada. Piña Colada, the perennial Caribbean treat, combines rum, coconut cream, and pineapple juice, in a drink so rich it seems more like a sweet. Rum serves as the base for many drinks.

There are fabulous inventions with names to match: "The Reverend's Downfall," a St. Lucia speciality, "Coco-Loco," and "El Dorado." If you're not careful, these sugary concoctions can give a mighty hangover.

Water from the tap is safe on all the islands. Mineral water is very highly priced.

HANDY TRAVEL TIPS

An A–Z Summary of Practical Information

A

AIRPORTS

Each of the major islands has an airport (St. Lucia has two) with varying facilities. See the Briefing sections under the various chapters. There are no porters in evidence at some airports. Some hotels provide courtesy cars.

Airport tax. You have to pay a fee upon departure, the price varying from island to island. The tax is usually less for inter-island trips than for destinations outside the Caribbean.

B

BICYCLE and MOTORCYCLE HIRE

Road conditions on most islands are not ideal for cycling or motorbike riding. Still, these can be rented in some places.

Barbados: For motorcycles or mopeds enquire at: Fun Seekers, Inc., Rockley Main Road, Christ Church; tel. 435-8206. You must be 21 or over and a licensed driver for at least two years. A visitor's permit is required (available for a small fee).

Several companies rent bicycles, including: Fun Seekers, Inc., and Williams Bicycle Rentals, Hastings, Christ Church; tel. 427-3955.

You must be 21 and in possession of a valid driver's license. A deposit is required. The cycle is insured, and personal accident insurance can be purchased for an extra fee.

BUSES

Buses are the only form of public transport on the islands but they are not always comfortable or fast. Barbados has the most modern fleet (blue and yellow) as well as a privately owned mini-bus service, both of which are quite efficient. Otherwise, all of the islands have modern, air-conditioned tour buses and mini-vans to provide local transportation.

C

CAMPING

There is a camp-site on Tobago at Canoe Bay Resort, with 50 places. If you try to sleep on the beaches (not permitted on Barbados), you may have to contend with insects, robbery, or even worse.

CARE HIRE (see also DRIVING)

Both international and local car hire firms operate on the major islands. During the high (winter) season, it is advisable to reserve a car in advance, especially on Trinidad-Tobago and Barbados. The Mini-Moke, a kind of jeep, is popular all over, especially on Barbados.

Prices and conditions vary considerably. Mini-Mokes are sometimes cheaper to rent than other models, and require less petrol (gasoline). If payment isn't made by credit card, a deposit up to US$1,500 is often required.

You must be 25 years old to rent a car, and show a valid driver's license (held for at least four years when renting from certain Trinidadian firms). On most islands (except Trinidad and Tobago, where you are required to have an International Driving Permit), drivers must purchase a visitor's driving permit from the local police station.

CLIMATE

Southern Caribbean temperatures rarely reach unbearable levels though humidity can be enervating in summer. Weather is best during the peak tourist season (December l5-April 15), with lower temperatures and less rain, but prices are higher. The official hurricane season is from June 1 to November 30, but only an average of six hurricanes blow through the Caribbean each year.

Trinidad is crowded during Carnival (usually in February, sometimes early March), but the fun and spectacle are worth it.

Average monthly temperatures for Barbados:

	J	F	M	A	M	J	J	A	S	O	N	D
°C	25	24	25	25	26	27	26	26	27	27	26	25
°F	77	75	77	77	79	81	79	79	81	81	79	77

CLOTHING

It's easy to pack for a Southern Caribbean holiday, since temperatures are high year-round. You'll need light clothing, preferably of cotton, which allows perspiration to evaporate more easily than synthetic fibres.

Informality is the keynote on the islands. Although clothing requirements vary from resort to resort, an elaborate wardrobe isn't necessary—even in the evening. Bustling Port-of-Spain is the only exception. Beach attire is, of course, unsuitable in towns and public places. Topless and nude bathing are prohibited on public beaches.

Be sure to bring walking, jogging, or tennis shoes, as well as rubber-soled footwear for beachcombing and snorkeling.

The islands are so warm that you hardly ever need much of a cover-up except, perhaps, in draughty air-conditioning. Take an umbrella for the warm rain that can fall between July and December (in Trinidad and Tobago the rainy season starts in May). Hikers should take a light waterproof parka, plus long trousers, long-sleeved shirts, and a hat.

Locally manufactured clothes can be reasonable in price, and tourists whose luggage has temporarily gone astray have been known to outfit themselves completely during a quick trip to town. All imported articles of clothing are fairly expensive.

COMMUNICATIONS

Post offices. On the larger islands postal service is generally good. Main post office addresses and hours:

Barbados: Cheapside, Bridgetown. Open 7:30 a.m. to 5 p.m. Monday to Friday.

St. Lucia: General Post Office, Bridge Street, Castries. Open 8:30 to 12 a.m., 1 to 4 p.m. weekdays only.

St. Vincent: General Post Office, Halifax Street, Kingstown. Open 8:30 a.m. to 3 p.m. Monday to Friday, 8:30 to 11:30 a.m. Saturday.

Grenada: General Post Office, Carenage, St. George's. Open 8:30 a.m. to 3:30 p.m. Monday to Thursday (to 4:30 p.m. Friday).

Trinidad: Main Post Office, Wrightson Road, Port-of-Spain. Open 7 a.m. to 5 p.m. Monday to Friday.

Tobago: Scarborough has a small post office, open during the week from 8 a.m. to 4:15 p.m. (Fridays 4 p.m.).

If you don't know in advance where you'll be staying, you can have mail sent to the Postmaster-General, General Delivery, at the central post office of the island in question. But you should first inform the post office, which will then keep your mail.

Stamps are sold in post offices and hotels, sometimes at small shops drugstores and mini-marts. Prices vary, but postage is very reasonable compared with rates elsewhere.

Telephone. Most public telephones are now card-phones, and cards are widely available in shops and post offices. The same card can be used on St. Lucia, St. Vincent, and the Grenadines, but Trinidad and Tobago each has its own system and their cards are not interchangeable.

Calls can be made through hotel operators, but charges are 3-4 times higher than the normal rates. International calls can easily be made from the main post offices, but you may have to wait, as only 25% of the population have their own telephones.

Telegrams, telex, fax. Most hotels will send telegrams; some have their own telexes. Night letter rates are usually cheaper. Main telex/telegram offices:

Barbados: Barbados External Telecommunications, Ltd., Carlisle House, Hinks Street, Bridgetown, tel. 426-3178. Open Monday to Friday 8 a.m. to 5 p.m., Saturday 8 a.m. to 1 p.m.; closed Sundays and public holidays. Another office, in Wildey, St. Michael, is open from 7 a.m. to 9 p.m. seven days a week.

St. Lucia: Cable and Wireless, Bridge Street, Castries, tel. 453-9000. Open 7 a.m. to 7 p.m. Monday to Saturday; closed Sundays and holidays.

St. Vincent: Cable and Wireless, Halifax Street, Kingstown, tel. 456 4998. Open 7 a.m. to 7 p. m. Monday to Saturday, 8 a.m to noon on Sunday and holidays.

Grenada: Cable and Wireless, Mercury House, Carenage, tel. 440-1000. Open 7 a.m. to 7 p.m. Monday to Saturday, 4 to 6 p.m. on Sunday and holidays.

Trinidad: TSTT, 54 Frederick Street, Port-of-Spain, tel. 624-5703. Open 24 hours a day for international fax, phone and internet services. On Trinidad and Tobago the major hotels also provide fax, phone and internet services. The main post offices have fax machines.

COMPLAINTS

If you feel you've been wronged, go first to the manager or owner of the establishment in question (restaurant, hotel, car hire agency, etc.). Your next resort is the local tourist board; for addresses, island by island, see Briefing section at the end of each chapter.

On certain islands, there are hotel associations which sort out hotel/restaurant complaints:

Barbados Hotel Association, 4th Avenue, Belleville, St. Michael, tel. 426-5041

Trinidad Hotels, Restaurants and Tourism Association, Airways Road, Chaguaramas, Trinidad, tel; 634-1174/75

Grenada Hotel and Tourism Association, P.O. Box 440, St. George's, tel. 444-1353

CRIME

As elsewhere, crime is on the rise in the Southern Caribbean. Take the usual precautions, and avoid bringing valuable jewellery to the islands. If you must, store it and other valuables (money, passport) in a hotel safe. Lock your room at all times, including the door that leads to the terrace. Do not leave valuables unattended on the beach.

The streets of the larger towns are best avoided at night, especially if you're alone or not accompanied by local people. Muggings and street theft, though infrequent, do occur. However romantic and tempting the beach may look after dark, do not venture out alone on certain parts of these islands. Ask your hotel bartender, reception clerk, or manager for advice before taking a late-night stroll.

CUSTOMS and ENTRY FORMALITIES

When you enter each island-nation, general duty-free rules apply. You may bring in about a quart or litre of wine or spirits, 200 cigarettes or 250 grams of tobacco, or up to 50 cigars, and any personal effects for immediate use as a tourist. The following chart shows which duty-free items you may bring back home with you:

Into:	Cigarettes		Cigars		Tobacco	Spirits		Wine
Australia	200	or	250g	or	250g	1*l*	or	1*l*
Canada	200	and	50	and	900g	1*l*	or	1*l*
N. Zealand	200	or	50	or	1/2 lb	1 qt	pr	1 qt
S. Africa	400	and	50	and	250g	1*l*	and	1*l*
U.K*.	200	or	50	or	250g	1*l*	and	2*l*
U.S.A.	200	and	100	and	**	1*l*	or	1*l*

* For items purchased in a duty-free shop.
** No restriction for personal use only.

Certain islands (Barbados, St. Lucia, St. Vincent, Grenada) do not require passports for citizens of the U.S., U.K., or Canada, though you must present a valid proof of citizenship (birth certificate, voter's registration card, etc.) But a passport is always the best identification, and is required on Trinidad-Tobago. Citizens of other countries must have passports, though the islands do not usually require visas (enquire at your tourist office or airline company). You must also present an ongoing or return ticket upon arrival on each island.

Yellow fever vaccination is no longer necessary for Barbados, Grenada, or St. Lucia. However, it is officially recommended on Trinidad and Tobago if you are arriving from an infected area.

Customs and immigration officials always ask how long you plan to stay on the island you're entering. You are usually allowed a visit of 3 to 6 months without a special visa. If you're travelling to Trinidad-Tobago, you must include both islands when you mention your length of stay. Be advised that changing a tourist visa in the Caribbean can be an administrative headache.

D

DRIVING

Shipping your own car to the islands is probably not worth the trouble. On the major islands there's no problem about hiring a car.

If you're a visitor to Trinidad and Tobago, you may drive on your own driving license—providing it is not temporary or provisional—for a period of 90 days. After that time, you must obtain an International Driving Permit from the nearest licensing office. All the other islands require you to purchase a temporary visitor's driving permit.

Driving conditions. As in Great Britain, driving is on the left. Roads are almost uniformly difficult compared to the U.S., U.K., or Canada. They can be narrow and pot-holed, with drainage ditches on either side. Mountain roads are full of hairpin bends, so it's a good idea to blow your horn before the bend. Watch out for pedestrians and animals in the road. You may also come upon an occasional lorry (truck) taking up too much of the available road space.

Road signs. There are several stop-lights on the larger islands, particularly in the capitals and smaller towns. Some international pictograph signs indicate stop, yield right-of-way, do not enter, etc., but these are not numerous. Nor are road signs (except on Barbados, where towns are relatively well marked). To find your way when driving, navigate with the best road maps you can buy. You might see a few signs in kilometres—this chart will help you make the conversion:

Parking regulations. Parking is allowed wherever there is space, except when specifically prohibited. There are several parking lots and two multi-storey car parks in Port-of-Spain, Trinidad. There are also a few car parks in Bridgetown, Barbados. In most other Caribbean towns you just have to look for a free space. There are no parking meters.

Speed limits. These are sometimes marked. In all built-up areas in Trinidad and Tobago, the speed limit is 50 km/h (just over 30 mph). On open roads, the limit is 80 km/h (50 mph). But you'll find that you cannot safely go much faster than 30 mph on most roads, and that town traffic generally moves along at about 25-35 km/h (15-20 mph). Note that speed limits, when posted, are strictly enforced on Barbados.

Breakdowns. Should misfortune occur, you'll usually have to rely on local people or the police for help. If you're hiring a car, the company is responsible for any problems you may have. The Trinidad and Tobago Automobile Association provides a breakdown service, limited to normal office hours.

Fuel. Prices vary, and, as elsewhere, are rapidly increasing But on Trinidad-Tobago, petrol (gasoline) will probably remain a bargain for a while, since Trinidad is a petroleum-producing country. Petrol is sometimes sold by the litre. Here are the various fluid-measure equivalents:

Fluid measures

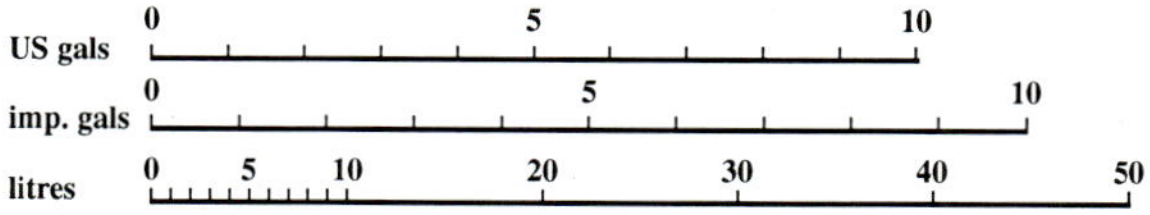

Distance

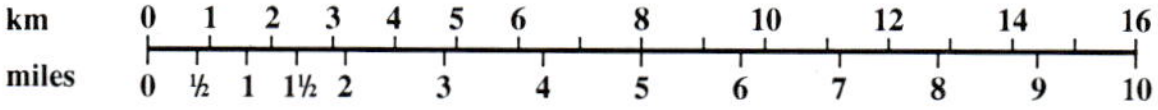

E

EMBASSIES, CONSULATES, HIGH COMMISSIONS

There are very few consular services on the islands. The largest offices are maintained on Barbados and Trinidad. Most countries are represented by honorary consuls (private citizens who will try to give assistance).

Barbados. Hours are roughly 8 a.m. to 4 or 5 p.m. Monday to Friday, with variations. If you are on an island without consular representation, you can ring Barbados if your country is represented here:

U.S.A.: United States Embassy, Canadian Imperial Bank of Commerce Building, Broad Street, Bridgetown, tel. 436-4950

U.K.: British High Commission Building, Collymore Rock, St. Michael, tel. 436-6694
Canada: Canadian High Commission, Bishop Court's Hill, Pine Road, St. Michael, tel. 429-3550

Trinidad. Opening hours are approximately 8 a.m. to 4:30 p.m. Monday to Friday. Some consulates close for a lunch break.
U.S.A.: United States Embassy, 15 Queen's Park West, Port-of-Spain, tel. 622-6371-6
U.K.: British High Commission, 19 St. Clair Avenue, Port-of-Spain, tel. 628-1234/2478
Canada: Canadian High Commission, Maple House, 3 Sweet Briar Road, Port-of-Spain, tel. 622-6232
St. Vincent has little in the way of consulates. The Deputy British High Commissioner can be reached in Kingstown, tel. 457-1701

G

GETTING THERE

Because of the complexity and variability of fares, you should ask the advice of an informed travel agent well before your departure.

From North America

BY AIR

Barbados: Regular non-stop service from Miami, New York, Montreal, and Toronto. Many connecting flights through San Juan.

St. Lucia: Regular non-stop service from Miami, New York, Washington, D.C., and Toronto. Many connecting flights through San Juan.

St. Vincent: You can reach St. Vincent by changing aircraft in Barbados or Port-of-Spain (Trinidad). The main gateways are Miami, New York, and San Juan.

Grenada: Regular non-stop service from Miami. Frequent connecting flights through San Juan.

Trinidad: Regular non-stop service from New York and Miami.

Package tours and charter flights. Sports programmes (golf, tennis, diving) are featured year-round. Many vacation packages are offered with or without car hire. If meals are not included in your package, the MAP (breakfast plus one other meal) plan is a money-saver.

BY SEA

The Southern Caribbean islands are favourite stops on cruises originating in Florida or Puerto Rico.

From Great Britain

BY AIR

Barbados: Direct service from Heathrow on two major carriers.

Trinidad: Regular non-stop service from Heathrow; other flights stop in Antigua or/and Barbados.

St. Lucia: Regular non-stop service from Heathrow; other flights stop in Barbados.

St. Vincent and Grenada: Fly to Barbados, Trinidad or St. Lucia, then change to a local air carrier. Weekly direct flight to Grenada.

Package tours: Package holidays are offered to one island or more in all price ranges.

BY SEA

Although passenger liners no longer sail directly to the Caribbean from Great Britain, cruise operators now fly tourists out to the islands or Miami to join their ship.

Many lines offer cruises to Barbados originating from Southampton England; Bremen, Germany; San Juan, Puerto Rico; New York; San Francisco, California; and Fort Lauderdale and Miami, Florida.

Between the islands

Local air service between the islands is excellent. Daily flights link the six major islands mentioned in this book, and in some cases service is almost hourly. For further information, including boat services, see INTER-ISLAND TRAVEL, page 118.

GUIDES

There are very few private tour guides, though small group tours can easily be arranged through agencies and hotels. Taxi drivers can be reliable guides. To find a good one, ask the tourist board or your hotel reception clerk.

H

HAIRDRESSERS and BARBERS

Most hairdressing establishments cater to both men and women. They can be found in the better hotels and on the main shopping streets of large towns. Prices vary, and will be higher, for example, in an exclusive Barbados hotel than in a small shop on St. Lucia.

HEALTH PRECAUTIONS

A sun tan can make you look wonderful but a bad burn could ruin your holiday and your skin, and increase the risk of skin cancer. So take it easy at first, especially if you have fair skin. Use sun-screen creams with a sun protection factor (SPF) of at least 15, and wear a hat. Start with a few minutes' exposure the first day, increasing gradually. The sun's burning rays are at their most powerful from 11:30 a.m. to 2:30 p.m. After a very hot day, a long night of air-conditioning could give you a chill or cold. If you need air-conditioning, put it on the "low" setting and keep out of the draft.

Food presents no special problems, though you might avoid street-stand snacks if you have a delicate stomach. Try not to mix sun, pills, and alcohol. When packing for your trip, don't forget an adequate supply of your favourite medications, including aspirin, an analagesic and something to soothe the stomach and combat diarrhea. In any event, local drugstores sell aspirin and home remedies (some reminiscent of the old patent-medicine days).

Insects. Mosquitoes, gnats, and sand flies are a prevalent nuisance, though not dangerous. Skin creams which repel insects are available at local pharmacies. You can burn mosquito coils in your hotel room if mosquitoes are a problem. If you request it, the maid will spray your room.

Manchineel tree. This tree, with its attractive but highly poisonous green fruit, is found all over the islands, especially near beaches. Even the bark and leaves are extremely toxic. Do not stand under the tree or touch the apple, which is poisonous. Most manchineel trees are clearly labelled or painted with a red ring.

Schistosomiasis parasite. Also called bilharzia, this parasite causes a highly dangerous illness that is crippling or deadly. The parasite is carried by snails that inhabit fresh-water ponds on St. Lucia and—to a lesser extent—some of the other islands. Always ask your guide or a local resident if ponds or streams are safe before bathing or wading. After exposure to the parasite, it may take several weeks for symptoms to develop. If you have flu with chest pains after visiting the islands, be sure to tell your doctor where you have been.

Urchins and coral. When in the water, take care to avoid the prickly black sea urchin. If you accidentally step on one, the best cure is to apply lime or lemon juice immediately. This helps to calcify the spines, which then work their way harmlessly out of the skin. Razor-sharp coral can pierce your skin in an instant, so wear tennis shoes or flippers when snorkeling. Treat coral cuts as you would any wound, with antiseptic, plus the healing power of fresh sea air. Avoid touching red coral, as it can give you a nasty stinging rash which lasts for days.

Snakes. The deadly *fer-de-lance* has been seen in the interior of the volcanic islands, but is hardly ever encountered by tourists.

Sharks. These do roam the Caribbean and Atlantic, but you probably won't see any. Avoid swimming at night, and don't wear shiny objects underwater.

HITCHHIKING

Some people hitchhike, and there is no law against it. But it's not recommended. Obviously, if you have a car and meet somebody at the beach who needs a lift, you should use your discretion.

HOTELS and ACCOMMODATION

Every sort of accommodation is available on the major islands, from the comfort of expensive luxury hotels to small, self-catering studio flats. Tourist boards and travel agents can furnish official lists.

Remember that high season rates (roughly December 15 to April 15) are considerably higher than prices from April to December. Reserve in advance, especially during high season. Tourist boards usually have a complete set of photo-brochures of the major hotels, plus lists of self-catering accommodation (not always that much of a saving, or very practical).

The various plans offered are:

EP: European Plan (room only)
CP: Continental Plan (room and breakfast)
AP: American Plan (room and three meals)
MAP: Modified American Plan (room, breakfast plus one other meal)

Some hotels allow only AP or MAP systems during high season. MAP is quite popular, since it saves money and is practical, unless you're set on trying a lot of restaurants.

In some hotels, package-tour deals offer lower rates for the same quality. Guest-houses are usually very reasonable, though there are fewer amenities. There are flats and small houses to let in all price ranges, and some of them are moderately priced. All accommodation except for the most luxurious is somewhat less expensive on St. Lucia, St. Vincent, and Grenada than on the other islands.

On all islands, taxes are charged in hotels and guest-houses, and there is usually a service charge as well. Trinidad and Tobago (currently the most expensive) adds on taxes of 15%, plus 10% service.

I

INTER-ISLAND TRAVEL

You can, of course, travel between the islands by hired yacht, complete with staff, food, Champagne, etc. Many hire companies have branch offices in the U.S. You can also hire a speedboat with driver.

Tour operators offer one- or two-day excursions using the local airlines. But if you'd like to get around by yourself:

From Trinidad to Tobago: There are several flights a day between Trinidad and Tobago (see Briefing page 79). There is also a ferry service; the trip takes between 5 and 8 hours and seas can be rough.

From St. Vincent to the Grenadines: Mustique, Canouan, Bequia, and Union Island have airstrips for small planes. Enquire at Arnos Vale Airport (St. Vincent) for scheduled, unscheduled, and charter flights. A daily shuttle schooner for tourists leaves Kingstown for Bequia in the afternoon, returning the next morning. This service is inexpensive and reliable. Ferries are also available to the other major Grenadine islands, though not on a daily basis. The adventurous can also travel through the Grenadines by mail boat. The boat leaves twice a week from Kingstown in the morning, stopping several times in the Grenadines and arriving at Grenada in the evening.

From Grenada to Carriacou and Petit Martinique: Daily 20-minute flights link Grenada and Carriacou. Trading schooners sail regularly from St. George's Harbour (Grenada) to Carriacou; from there you can sail on to Petit Martinique (just 3 miles to the northeast).

L

LANGUAGE

The official language on all the islands covered in this book is English, spoken in a variety of accents. If you don't understand what's being said, just ask. The person you're talking to will repeat more clearly. On St. Lucia (and to some extent on St. Vincent) the people speak a lilting French patois among themselves.

LAUNDRY and DRY-CLEANING

Hotels can take care of laundry efficiently. One-day service is always possible, but costs more. There are no launderettes except on Barbados, though some towns have quick-service laundry and dry-cleaning establishments (not necessarily cheaper than the hotels).

Prices vary according to where you are—they are usually higher on Barbados, lower on Tobago, Grenada, St. Vincent, and St. Lucia.

LOST PROPERTY

For lost property, ask at the hotel or establishment where you misplaced the item. If you've left something on a bus, check with the local transport board. As a last resort, you could try the police station.

M

MAPS

Sometimes hotels furnish basic maps free, and tourist boards usually do so as well. The quality of maps varies according to the country. The St. Vincent tourist board charges a small fee for a topnotch survey map. The Trinidad-Tobago tourist boards also have very good maps. A general map of St. Lucia is available in bookstores, and the tourist board gives out a small map. On Barbados, good tourist maps are available from the tourist board in Bridgetown and hotels or for a fee in the tourist section of the local shops.

MEDICAL CARE (See also Briefing section under each island for emergencies, hospital)

The islands have adequate to good medical facilities and physicians, especially on Barbados. Hotels or the tourist board can recommend a doctor or dentist. You can also look in the classified section of the phone book. Chemists' (pharmacy) opening hours vary; some are open several days a week, though there is almost no 24-hour service. For pharmacies open in the evening, ask at your hotel desk or consult the local newspaper or phone book.

Here are a few pharmacies usually open after regular hours:

Trinidad: Alchemists' Drug Store, 57 Duke Street, Port-of-Spain, tel. 623-2718

Tobago: Dove Drugs, Burnett Street, Scarborough, tel. 639-2976

St. Lucia: Regis' Pharmacy, Morne du Don Road, Castries, tel. 452-3279

Grenada: Gitten's, Halifax Street, St. George's, and Grand Anse, tel. 440-2340 after hours. Duty free shop, tel. 440-3174

MONEY MATTERS

Currency. Various currencies are in use on the islands. See the Briefing section at the end of each chapter.

Banks and currency exchange. The general rule is that banks are open from 8 a.m. to noon or 1 p.m. weekdays, later on Friday afternoons. Banks often shut for a half-day before major holidays. For specific hours, see island Briefings. Banks almost always have currency exchange windows.

The most acceptable form of payment is U. S. (or Canadian) dollars in traveller's cheques. You will usually need a passport or driver's license for identification. Traveller's cheques are negotiable almost anywhere. Banks give the best rate of exchange, but in many cases you can get almost as good a rate at your hotel desk. Enquire as to how the rate compares with the bank's; hotels usually give an honest answer.

Credit cards and traveller's cheques. Major credit cards are widely accepted throughout the islands by most hotels, better restaurants, and shops, including duty-free shops at the airports (depending on the airport and type of purchase). Traveller's cheques are also accepted preferably those in U. S. dollars.

Prices. As elsewhere, inflation is on the rise. However, prices are still reasonable compared with big cities in the U.S., Canada, and Europe or European resort towns. In general, Barbados tends to be more expensive than the other islands in the area. Trinidad is now a more economical tourist destination than it used to be.

There are some extraordinary bargains, such as petrol (gasoline) on Trinidad-Tobago. Beware of French wines, which can cost more than spirits and a lot more than local rum. Some locally made beers are also quite good and inexpensive.

Hotels and restaurants vary in price, but generally you'll find that for higher prices you do get better quality. Visiting the islands on package deals and especially during the low season (April 15-December 15) can mean considerable savings.

PLANNING YOUR BUDGET

To give you an idea of what to expect, here's a sampling of average prices. They can only be approximate, however, as inflation creeps relentlessly up.

Airport departure tax. From *Barbados* BD$25, from *Trinidad* TT$75, from *St. Vincent* EC$20, from *St. Lucia* EC$27 to Caribbean islands, EC$20 to other destinations.

Buses. *Barbados* any one-way trip BD$1.50, *Grenada* EC$1-5.

Car hire. *Barbados,* Mini-Moke BD$110 per day. *St. Lucia*, $60-70 a day, $220-300 a week.

Cigarettes. *Barbados.* BD$4.50-6.00 per packet of 20.

Driving. Temporary permit, *Barbados* BD 10, *St. Lucia* EC$30, *St. Vincent* EC$40, Grenada EC$30.

Entertainment (night-club cover charge). *Barbados* BD$10.

Ferry. From *Trinidad to Tobago*, Economy TT$25 one way; from *Grenada to Carriacou* US$7.50 one way.

Hairdressers and barbers. *Barbados,* wash and blow-dry BD$30, man's cut BD$20. *Trinidad,* shampoo and set TT$20-40, man's cut TT$10-20.

Hotels. High season, double room with bath, MAP per person. *Barbados* luxury from US$430 per day plus 15% (tax and service), average from US 130 per night plus 15%.

Motorcycle hire. *Barbados.* US$28-58 per day, US$145-289 per week.

Taxis. *Barbados,* from airport to central Bridgetown BD$15. *Trinidad,* from airport to Port-of-Spain TT$100.

P

PETS

Few people bring pets on Caribbean holidays, due to strict government regulations. On Barbados, for example, visiting animals must undergo six months of quarantine before being allowed into the country.

PHOTOGRAPHY

You can buy major brands of film, but it's best to bring your own, since supplies can be limited and prices are high. There are fast-development services on the larger islands, especially for black-and-white and transparencies. But in most cases, development is cheaper back home.

To ensure good colour transparencies in the blazing sunlight, you must use a skylight or similar filter. You'll probably get best seashore and outdoor results late in the afternoon.

Local people (especially children) are usually cooperative about having their pictures taken. But always ask first, and offer some small change if it seems this would be appreciated. Some people react in a hostile way if you try to photograph them. Islanders are proud, and you should respect their dignity.

Be sure to enquire whether security checks are made by X-ray, which can be harmful to undeveloped film.

POLICE

Each town, city, and parish on the islands has a police station, and local people can always direct you to the nearest one. Police uniforms are "British-tropical," usually navy-blue trousers or shorts, grey shirts and white safari hats, or helmets. The harbour police of Barbados dress in costumes right out of Gilbert and Sullivan. Once in a while you might spot a policeman directing traffic, but this is a rare sight on the islands. For police phone numbers, see various Briefing sections.

R

RADIO and TV

Most radio programmes are in English. In addition to local offerings, programmes from Canada, the U.S. and BBC are broadcast on medium- or short-wave frequencies. A few French programmes from Martinique are transmitted to other islands.

All islands now have their own TV stations. There is a general diet of aged U.S. repeats and locally made chat shows. There is also U.S. cable television, and most hotels have U.S. satellite TV. Radio and

TV stations are generally government-operated, and shows feature local political chit-chat, some international news, and music. Radios in hotel rooms pick up a few local stations with a limited selection of music. Some of the higher-class hotels have TV sets.

RELIGIOUS SERVICES

Anglicans and Roman Catholics are in the majority on the islands. Methodist, Baptist, and Seventh-Day Adventist churches, Hindu temples, synagogues, and mosques point out the diversity of faiths in the Caribbean, especially on Trinidad and Barbados. For addresses and times of services, check with local newspapers, your hotel desk, or the tourist office.

T

TAXIS

As there are no meters, you should agree on a price with your driver before taking a taxi. In principle, taxi fares are set by the government of each island according to the mileage covered, in practice, you might hear some rather varied fares for the same distance on the same island. Before taking a taxi, ask at your hotel desk about the correct fare. You can also consult the tourist board office or the airport information officer before taking a taxi to a hotel.

Taxis are not always indicated as such, but you'll probably recognize drivers frequenting promising locations. On some islands, the word "taxi" is clearly marked on the windshield (windscreen). On Barbados, taxi license plates have a small number 591 in addition to the regular number, and taxis carry signs which are lit at night to indicate that the taxi is on duty. On other islands, you will see "H" (for hire car) on the plate.

Drivers often double as guides. If you want to be sure of having a good one, reserve a day or so in advance through your hotel desk or the tourist office. You don't have to tip taxi drivers, though a 10 per cent tip is always appreciated, especially if your driver has been giving you advice or acting as a guide. The shared-taxi service that operates around Port-of-Spain on Trinidad and on Tobago proves a lot less expensive than a regular taxi. There are certain designated stops, be sure to signal the taxi when you see it approaching.

TIME DIFFERENCES

The islands stay on Atlantic Standard Time all year. This is one hour ahead of Eastern Standard Time and four hours behind GMT. The U.S. east coast and the islands are on the same time when Daylight Savings Time is in effect.

Winter

Los Angeles	Chicago	New York	**Islands**	London
8 a.m.	10 a.m.	11 a.m.	**noon**	4 p.m.

TIPPING

A 10 percent service charge is often included in hotel and restaurant bills. If not added to bills, tip the waiter 10-15 percent. Taxi drivers also get 10-15 percent, bellboys and porters about U.S.$1 per bag.

TOILETS

There are very few public facilities on the islands. They're usually marked "public conveniences" with a silhouette or a sign indicating "men" or "women."

Airports always have toilet facilities, but not all of them are inviting.

W

WATER

Tap water in hotels, restaurants and flats is safe on all the islands. It tastes quite good, especially on Barbados. The islands sometimes have problems with plumbing, in which case water in hotel rooms may be turned off. The hotel will give you safe drinking water if this happens. You can buy bottled mineral water, but it is rather expensive.

INDEX